William Bright

Some Aspects of Primitive Church Life

William Bright

Some Aspects of Primitive Church Life

ISBN/EAN: 9783337162337

Printed in Europe, USA, Canada, Australia, Japan

Cover: Foto ©Lupo / pixelio.de

More available books at **www.hansebooks.com**

SOME ASPECTS

OF

PRIMITIVE CHURCH LIFE

BY

WILLIAM BRIGHT, D.D.

REGIUS PROFESSOR OF ECCLESIASTICAL HISTORY, AND CANON OF
CHRIST CHURCH, OXFORD

LONGMANS, GREEN, AND CO.
39 PATERNOSTER ROW, LONDON
NEW YORK AND BOMBAY
1898

All rights reserved

ADVERTISEMENT

THE following Addresses were for the most part delivered, in a somewhat less expanded form, at a "Summer Meeting of Clergy" in Oxford.

CHRIST CHURCH,
October 21, 1898.

CONTENTS

ADDRESS I.

Introduction—Early Christians a Puzzle to Pagans—External likeness to a Guild—Was the Apostolic Church formed by Self-aggregation?—The New Testament represents it as a special Divine creation—Was it also Divinely provided with an Organization?—Did Christ institute a Ministry by empowering an Apostolate?—The negative view inconsistent with New Testament language—Theory of "Apostolic Commission" to the whole Christian Society—Subsequent action of the Twelve as Apostles and Church Rulers—The Apostolic "background"—Appointment of the Seven—St. Paul, called to the Apostleship, acts as a Ruler—St. James, "the Lord's brother," Apostolic Ruler at Jerusalem—Provision made for the Future—A Local Ministry—"Presbyters" also known as "Episkopoi"—Presbyters left in charge at Ephesus, afterwards placed under Timothy—Timothy, at first Apostolic Deputy, then sole Chief Pastor—"Evangelists and Prophets"—"Angels of Seven Churches"—St. John and Episcopacy—St. Clement of Rome—The "Tunnel" Period—St. Ignatius—Settlement of Episcopacy gradual—Dignity of Presbyters under Bishops—Episcopacy a True Development—Retrospect to Christ's Words—Two Theories of Ministry 1

ADDRESS II.

Apostolic Rule not Despotic—St. Paul's line of action—Council of Jerusalem—Harmony of Pastors and People—Sympathy and Confidence—A Sense of Common Interest—General and Special Priesthood—St. Clement's Epistle—His reference to the Laity—Import of the term—Presbyters "offering"—Ignatius on Ministration—Tertullian, as a Montanist, on Lay priesthood—Questionable as a witness to Catholic usage—His estimate of Ministrations—"Prophesying" in Apostolic age—Cases of Lay

Preaching—Lay interest in Discipline—Laymen resisting the relaxation of Rules—Lay right in appointments of Bishop and Clergy—Weight attached to Lay Testimony—Relation of Laity to Synods—Influence without Membership—Bishops amid their People—Episcopate in third Century an office of Chief Rule—Despotism excluded by Church-idea—Cyprian's principle of action—The Mind of the Laity ascertained as to the Lapsed—The later Question as to Heretics' Baptism—Less of a Layman's Question than the earlier one—Yet Laymen were present at its Synodical decision—Primitive status of Laity unlike modern Roman, but also unlike Anglican under Conditions of Establishment—Practical Difficulty of defining a "Layman" 51

ADDRESS III.

The Sacramental Principle—Primitive Idea of Baptism—Its Administration—Confirmation—The Holy Eucharist—Time of its Celebration—Its Relation to the "Agape"—Ignatius on Agape and Eucharist—Justin Martyr on the Eucharist—Irenæus on the Eucharist—The Twofold Liturgy—Various Ritual Indications—Keeping the Sacrament at Home—The Lord's Day not a Sabbath—Weekly Fast-days—Paschal Controversy—Paschal Controversy: its First and Second Stages—Irenæus and Victor—Sacraments and a Divine Christ—Belief in Christ Doctrinal—St. Paul's Attitude towards Christ—The Sub-apostolic Church not "Humanitarian"—Two Classes of Ebionites—Early Christology unsystematic—Problem of correlating the Trinity with the Unity—Both Truths practically combined—Effect of the Faith on Conduct—Moral Improvement vast, but not without Drawbacks—Secularising Influences—Apostles "retaining Sins"—Penitential Discipline involving Public Confession—Idealising set apart, the Fruits witness for the Tree—Evidence of Characters purified and ennobled—Seriousness of tone with Joyousness of spirit—These Results due to the "Thought of Christ"—Ordinary Life hallowed—Practical Charity and Equity—Energetic Horror of Vice—Christians a "Remnant"—Spread of Christian Influence 100

ADDRESS IV.

Conversions not due to a mere Craving for "Wonders"—Pagan Credulity not attracted by a Christ—Idolatry ubiquitous: Difficulty of keeping aloof from it—Cases of Conscience in Various Occupations—Public Amusements heathenish or demoralising—Christians called disaffected—Temptation to compromise—Mob-fury under a Panic—Libels against Christians widely current—Educated Pagans as intolerant as the Vulgar—Persecution by the Populace—Principle of Official Persecution—Christianity treated as "illicit," at first on Political grounds—Nero's Barbarities might form a Precedent—Domitian's acts of Persecution—Policy of later Emperors—St. Peter on the "Fiery Trial"—Limited Persecutions—Decian Persecution General—Christians before the Tribunal—Magistrates using Persuasion to obtain Compliance—Previous Relaxation of Tone resulting in Apostasy—Imprisonment and Torture—Martyrs—Impressiveness of Martyrdom—Enthusiasm for Martyrs—Value of their Example—Question of Flight from Persecution—Evasive Expedients—"Libellatics"—Good Effects of Persecution 153

ADDRESS V.

"Apology" a task for the Church—Hints from St. Paul as to its Fulfilment—Appeal to "Moral Reason"—The First Apologists—Justin on the Word as the Guide of Humanity—Value of his Idea—Epistle to Diognetus—The Incarnation and Atonement—Tatian—Athenagoras—Theophilus—Clement of Alexandria as Writer and Teacher—His Spiritual Earnestness—His Theological Defects—Not sufficiently Pauline; too much of an Idealist—His Special Merits as an Apologist—Origen—Celsus against Christianity—He adopts Jewish Objections—Origen's Reply—His openly Pagan Attack, and Origen's Reply—Valuable Characteristics of Origen's Apology—Minucius Felix—Pagan Case represented—Octavius' Reply—Appeal to Philosophy—Vindication of Christian Conduct—The Pagan half-converted—Idolatry linked with Vice—Tertullian—His Faults as an Arguer—Appeal of Christianity to Man as Man—Christian Social Life—Recognition of Civil Duty—Spread of Christianity—"Apology" in Practical Form 200

ADDITIONAL NOTE 255

INDEX 263

ERRATA

Page 68, line 5 from bottom, *for* 413 *read* 113.
,, 93, ,, 7, *for* "as a reverent crowd" *read* as "a reverent crowd."
,, 98, last line, *for* doctrines *read* doctrine.
,, 111, *note* 1, *for* scene *read* sense.
,, 143, ,, 2, *for* Aznobius *read* Arnobius.
,, 220, ,, 3, *for* Stores *read* Stoics.
,, 257, line 1 *for* 23 *read* 33.

ADDRESS I.

For the purpose of these addresses it must suffice to look at certain aspects of primitive Church history in their general outline. The field is very wide, and we can only traverse parts of it: and even in regard to the subjects on which we can dwell, a full discussion of many details would be out of place, would more than fill up the time at our disposal. Our aim must be to form or to recover such ideas of the Church life of those distant "first centuries" as may afterwards admit of further illustrations, and may not require to be cast aside as determined by an erroneous standpoint.

Our first question may be stated thus: What was the primitive Church like as a community? In other words, we may try to see generally what was its constitution, to understand the forces which held it together, its official administration, the rights and duties of its ordinary members. We may next consider its observances, its beliefs, and the type of character which it originated and maintained. We may then look outwards, and endeavour to realise its position in regard to the huge encircling masses of non-Christian social life, and to the ruling powers of the Roman empire, central or provincial. And lastly, we may ask what methods it took to commend its case to such outsiders as were ready, or might be induced, to judge it fairly,—or even to advance from equity to sympathy, and so from sympathy to acceptance;—a work especially befitting the trained apologist, but still one in which all members of the Church were commanded by an Apostle to take part according to their opportunities and capacities,[1] in fulfilment of

---

[1] 1 Pet. iii. 15.

the great universal obligation to "fight the noble fight of the faith," and witness for the Saviour and King of men.[1]

(1.)

To begin, then, with the first part of the first question: the light that we want is but very partially attainable *ab extra*. We must, as it were, get inside the house, in order to understand how it is constructed and managed, what sort of persons are its inmates, how they spend their time, what use they make of their dwelling. To the average non-Christian observer, in the second or even the third century, the Christian society must have been a puzzling phenomenon. One can imagine that in many a Greek agora, at many a public meeting-place, in the baths where long summer days

[1] On the other controversies of the early Church something has been said in the writer's Waymarks in Church History.

were spent, at supper-parties in luxurious patrician homes, the question would repeatedly be asked, with a sort of irritation stirred by perplexity: "Can any one give us authentic information about these Christians? What *is* their religion? and what do they mean by keeping so much aloof from us? Are they as bad as Tacitus thought, when he branded Christianity as a 'pestilent superstition;' or are they harmless fanatics who had best be left to their own folly, instead of being periodically hunted down as atheists or misanthropists, conspirators, or bad subjects? One has heard very blackening rumours about their secret practices, but is there really much evidence to go upon?"[1] Such queries might call forth various replies, more or less conjectural: the uncertainty

---

[1] "Nescio an falsa," says the pagan in Minucius Felix's Octavius, 9; "certe occultis ac nocturnis sacris apposita suspicio." When Origen wrote, the worst libels against Christians were discredited, except among a few (c. Cels. vi. 27, 40). Cp Euseb. iv. 7.

would continue to exercise curiosity; and we know that it found expression in the nickname of "a third race of men,"[1] a class of beings, as we might say, who have to be ranked by themselves, being unlike everybody else — a sneer comparable to the Continental sarcasm which divides the race into "men, women, and clergy." That they were in some sense a visible body, with such organisation as was compatible with their circumstances, was clear enough: and this would be further ascertained when, for purposes of their own, the Christians assumed the character of one of those guilds which the Roman law called "colleges."[2] But who

[1] Tertullian, ad Nationes, i. 8.

[2] This expedient would be resorted to in the second century by way of facilitating the undisturbed burial of Christians—for many of the "collegia" were, in fact, burial societies, composed of mechanics or domestics, possessed of burial-places of their own, enlivened by periodical guild-suppers, and exempted from that prohibition of "clubs" which was part of the policy of Trajan. The monthly contributions, which, with entrance-fees, secured a certain allowance for each

originally formed this peculiar guild? We, of course, should answer, "The original disciples of Christ." The book of Acts, if we admit it to be even substantially genuine, is the earliest record of Church history: the Pauline epistles, read with it, will tell us a good deal as to what sort of society was that which we know as the Apostolic Church.[1] And if we accept this New Testament account of things, we must reject, from the Scriptural point of view, a theory which

---

member's own funeral, would be analogous to the contributions made by Christians in Africa on a certain day in each month, for charitable purposes, including the burial of the poor (Tertull., Apol. 39. Cp. Lanciani, Pagan and Christian Rome, p. 116; and Bishop Lightfoot, Dissertations on the Apostolic Age, p. 152). But it is one thing to say that the Church utilised this form of association, and quite another to say that her own existence was an imitation of it. The case of rich Christians allowing their fellow-Christians to be interred in their family burial-places was different, and gave rise to the formation of "catacombs" (cp. Allard, Hist. des Persécutions, ii. 467 ff.).

[1] It is too late by many centuries to attempt to naturalise the Hellenistic use of *Ecclesia*.

traces the Church to the voluntary aggregation of individuals united by a common devotion to Christ. Many a religious association has owed its existence to the coming together of a few persons, perhaps only two or three: they find that they are like-minded; they fraternise; they feel that it would be helpful to co-operate; they form a little band which grows by new adhesions, which may have a very useful, or even a great and beneficent career. The process is both natural and supernatural; religious minds see the over-ruling Hand stretched over it, acknowledge in its working the guidance of God's Spirit as the Author of "all good counsels," and say that its development is, in a serious and adequate sense, "Divine."[1] Now, is this a true account of the "genesis" of the Church? Not according to the Gospel account of "the kingdom of God," or "of heaven," as becoming present on earth

[1] Cp. Hatch, Bampton Lectures, ed. 1, p. 209.

in the personal ministry of Jesus Christ, and as destined to result in, and to express itself by, what we call a visible Church. We may now assume that the "invisible Church" idea does not come out of the Scripture documents: it is less frequently read into them than was once, not so long ago, the case.[1] They show us a Church discernible as an institution, or, if we prefer the word, an organism,—as St. Paul terms it, a body. It begins to live at the great Pentecost: so many, day after day, are "added to it": but it is not like a combination of individuals who, in a spirit of prayer and faith, coalesce for religious purposes into a "society," as other men form clubs, political, literary, or social.[2] Rather, in the well-known words

[1] The notion "that St. Paul regarded membership of the universal *Ecclesia* as invisible and exclusively spiritual ... seems to me incompatible with any reasonable interpretation of St. Paul's words" (Dr. Hort, The Christian Ecclesia, p. 169).

[2] "The Church is something more than ... a voluntary aggregation of individual souls for religious purposes.

of our present Primate,[1] "throughout the teaching of the Apostles we see that it is the Church which comes first, and the members of it afterwards." This may sound paradoxical, but it means that the converts regard the Church as constituted by a Divine act, as "flowing out from the Lord," and are "called into it:" they do not make it, they find it made for them. The distinction has a far-reaching import; and it has apparently been admitted [2] that those who believe Christ to have in this sense formed the Church, instead of allowing it to form itself, are quite consistent in believing that He also instituted a ministry, instead of leaving it to "evolve" or invent offices or polities for itself, as its varying needs might from time to

... The Church is an external society, an external brotherhood, an external kingdom, constituted by a Divine order. It has its laws, it has its officers" (Bishop Lightfoot, Ordination Addresses, p. 35).

[1] Sermon by Archbishop (then Bishop) Temple, at the consecration of Truro Cathedral.

[2] Cp. Hatch, Bamp. Lect., ed. 2, p. xii.

time suggest. But now it seems that the latter proposition is rejected by some who accept the former. We are told that to suppose Him so to have "trusted His Church"—the presence of the Holy Spirit being assumed—involves "a loftier conception" of its nature and capacities than to suppose that He Himself had provided it with an organisation. But this depends on the view we take of organisation in regard to that "one body" which "is Christ's." The word may, to some ears, be suggestive of what is formal and external—necessary indeed, like a "committee of management," for the working order of the society,—but still, so to speak, related only to its outside. But the religion of the Incarnation has taught us to see in form the vehicle of spirit; and wherever in the Christian domain there is antagonism between the inward and outward, there is, *pro tanto*, failure.[1] The dispensation of the

[1] See the second chapter of Dr. Moberly's Ministerial Priesthood.

Redeemer's word and sacraments is bound up with interests vitally spiritual, and deeply embedded within the economy of His grace: it comes under that principle which St. Paul laid down when he spoke of the original agencies set in motion at Pentecost as "gifts" from the ascended Christ "for the full equipment of His holy ones, for a work of ministry, for the building up of His body," which is the Church.[1] And this term "gifts" has a deep significance, as illustrative of the great Christian principle of dependence on Divine bounty.[2] Is it not, then, at least supposable that our conceptions will be raised and not lowered, enriched and not impoverished, when we regard the Church as endowed with a human instrumentality analogous to that which we recognise in its

---

[1] Eph. iv. 12.
[2] Cp. Gladstone, Church Principles, etc., p. 224, on "the religious dispensation under which we live as a system of powerful influences emanating altogether from God, and operating upon us as their necessitous recipients;" and Gore, The Ministry, p. 77 ff.

sacraments; that it will seem, with good reason, all the more "fitly framed together" for possessing such tokens of the providence of its Head?[1]

(2.)

So that we are perforce driven back on the old inquiry: Did Christ institute a ministry for His Church? An eminent writer, in a posthumously published volume, which is in several respects both stimulating and suggestive, holds in effect that He did not. The Twelve, we are told, were essentially typical "disciples;"[2] up to the time of His

---

[1] If the "officers" of a "Kingdom of Christ" must, as such, have the function of "exhibiting Him to men, it would seem reasonable to expect that" as He Himself, "when upon earth, received a formal and outward designation to the office which He had undertaken," so "an equally formal and visible designation would bear witness to men that those offices which are fulfilled for their sakes . . . are held from Christ and under Christ," etc. (F. D. Maurice, Kingdom of Christ, ii. 144).

[2] They *were* so, and St. John always calls them so,—which shows that he is thinking of Apostles in xx. 19; but

death¹ they were only "Apostles" during a brief circuit among Galilæan villages; even after His Resurrection they received no special authority; their unique position as "witnesses" for Him could not but give them a kind of authority, but, though "lofty," it was "ill defined" and purely "moral," and rested on no grant from Himself.² It is

such discipleship, in proportion as it was realised, would be just what would fit them to be set over others.

[1] Dr. Hort is a little inconsistent here. From p. 24 ff. of his Christian Ecclesia, we gather that apostleship (proper) was in abeyance between the "return" of the Twelve in Mark vi. 30, Luke ix. 10, and "the Ascension." In pp. 36, 37, the inauguration of a "new apostolic mission" is placed "between the Resurrection and the Ascension;" and this again is further modified in p. 40, where the inauguration is dated from "the Crucifixion, interpreted, as always, by the Resurrection." This should be remembered in regard to Dr. Hort's view (see below), that the words of mission in John xx. 21, spoken with exceptional solemnity on the evening after the Resurrection, and when the print of nails and spear had just been exhibited, were not really meant for the Apostles, as such, at all.

[2] Hort, pp. 83–85, 230. St. Ignatius evidently thought otherwise: "I do not give you injunctions, as did Peter and Paul: *they* were Apostles" (Ep. Rom. 4; cp. Trall. 3).

clear, then, that we have got behind the question of apostolic succession to the question of an apostolic delegation, of any proper apostolic office. Dr. Hort broadly avers that "*there is no trace in Scripture of a formal commission of authority for government from Christ Himself*" to the Apostles as an order, as a body within the Church.[1] This negation goes a long way: it (1) obscures the significance of that elaborate training of the Twelve which was kept up to the very close of Christ's own ministry, for the purpose of making them the "organ" for the "distribution" of "Divine gifts"[2] amid wider and wider circles; (2) puts a strain on several momentous passages, such as the

---

[1] Hort, p. 84. Of course character may give "moral authority," but this will be the stronger for the substratum of a Divine commission. Take away that substratum, and the "authority" will have a merely subjective source, and be liable to indefinite variation. Cp. Liddon, Clerical Life and Work, p. 218 ff. ("The Moral Value of a Mission from Christ").

[2] H. S. Holland, Creed and Character, p. 63.

promise of the "keys,"—the promise of authority to bind and to loose (which we may describe as legislative),[1]—the promise, or announcement of an intention, on "the Lord's" part, to "set over His household" a *permanent* "stewardship" for the purpose of dispensing spiritual "food in due season,"[2]

[1] Dr. Hort quotes Matt. xvi. 19, but avoids "going into details of interpretation" (p. 19). In Matt. xviii. 17 he takes the ἐκκλησία to mean "the Jewish local community, to which the injured person and the offender both belonged" (p. 10). But such an interpretation would not fit in with the next words, in which the authority to bind and loose is again promised; and in the verse immediately following, "two of you," or "two or three," are contemplated as "agreeing to ask of the Father," or as "gathered together in the name" of His Son.

[2] Luke xii. 42; Matt. xxiv. 45 is identical in meaning, although it has "servant" instead of "steward." It is really surprising that these cardinal texts are not discussed by Dr. Hort. The idea of a steward in a palace is set forth in Isa. xxii. 20 ff; cp. 1 Kings iv. 6; xviii. 3. A delegated "rule" over the servants in general, analogous to, and involved in, the control over household stores, was essential to the function. Cp. Gen. xxiv. 2; xli. 40. The idea that the servants as a body could of themselves appoint a steward for their lord, is out of the question; and a functionary commissioned simply by the "Christian people" would not

—the illustrative mention of "the authority given to the householder's servants,"[1]—the implicit assertion that Judas, up to the moment of his "fall," held an office of "overseership," literally "episcopate"[2]—the great plenary mission on Easter-night,—the restoration, as it has been understood, of pastoral office to the Apostle who had forfeited it by his "denials;" and of these texts, it must be said, very insufficient account is taken in Dr. Hort's chapter on "The Apostles in Relation to the *Ecclesia*." Most of them are, in fact, passed over; but it is essential to his argument that the awful affirmation, "As the Father has sent Me, even so I send you,"

be a "minister of Christ," "of reconciliation," or "of the new covenant," in the Pauline sense of the phrases. Cp. 1 Cor. iv. 1, 2; 2 Cor. iii. 6. The use of the singular, "steward," creates no difficulty; for the one "household" is present in every organised local "church."

[1] Mark xiii. 34.

[2] Acts i. 20. In p. 211, Dr. Hort says, "Assuredly the ἐπισκοπή of the elders would count as an ἀρχή or government," as distinct from a διακονία. Why not, then, the ἐπισκοπή of an Apostle?

should be interpreted as addressed to "the whole *Ecclesia* of the future," through the Ten who for the time "represented" it.[1] But "we cannot have just as much of an argument as we like, and no more;" and Dr. Hort seems hardly to realise the consequence of this interpretation. On his showing, all apostleship whatever, in the fullest reach of any such term, was then and there, absolutely and irrevocably, made over to, and lodged in, the whole body of believers.

[1] Hort, p. 33. Dr. Hort argues that at the Last Supper the Twelve were simply "representatives of the *Ecclesia* at large" (p. 30); but the words in 1 Cor. xi. 24 (not to say Luke xxii. 19), especially when read in the light of the "steward" text, suggest that, besides being communicants, they were also bidden to "do" what they had seen Christ do in regard to the elements. And Dr. Hort, while quoting John xvii. 18 as meaning that "the whole *Ecclesia* shares alike in that transmitted mission" (p. 32), forgets that it *precedes* the transition of thought from "these," the Apostles then present, to "those that believe through their word;" so that it is precisely *not* "the whole *Ecclesia*," but the Eleven, that are there spoken of as "sent forth into the world"—a consideration which might of itself decide the interpretation of John xx. 21.

Thenceforward there was to be, there could be, but one true Apostle of Christ, the Christian people at large; and therefore, St. Peter, St. John, and the rest of the Ten, or rather Eleven, were *ipso facto* denuded of any special apostolic *status*; and as the word of Christ "was not yea and nay," we cannot suppose that He would have restored what by hypothesis He had so deliberately withdrawn.[1] Yet in the very next chapter of that same Fourth Gospel we find Him committing to one of the Apostles—by way, as we have seen, of reinstatement—a pastoral office, to be exercised towards and over the Christian people, and so worded as to involve

---

[1] Dr. Hort says, indeed, that after the Resurrection they received a "renewed apostleship" (p. 40), with a charge to preach to all nations, and to witness for Christ as risen. But on his interpretation of John xx. 21 this new charge would not be properly apostolic. Yet he feels obliged to say that "the apostolate of the Twelve and St. Paul was in an important sense a definite and permanent *office*" (p. 160). In what sense, and under what sanction?

a power of "government."[1] If we go on into the Acts we hear this same Apostle exhorting the hundred and twenty to pray that the Lord would show which of two persons He had chosen to fill a vacant "Apostleship;"[2] we see the Twelve, their number thus completed, acting not only as the nucleus, the central and formative element, of the infant community—its "bond of unity," in Dr. Hort's phrase,[3]—but as its teachers, leaders, directors.[4] As Dr. Moberly puts it,

[1] Ποίμαινε, John xxi. 16, may be illustrated by Matt. ii. 6, and by Ezekiel's use of "shepherds" for temporal rulers. In a very noble sermon in Dr. Hort's volume (p. 243), "tend" is explained as implying "government."

[2] This, soon after He had "spoken to the Apostles whom He had chosen" on "the things concerning the kingdom of God."

[3] Dr. Hort says (p. 168) that, "the members which make up the one *Ecclesia* are not communities, but individual men," etc. But "the members of all partial *Ecclesiæ*" are not regarded by St. Paul as individual units. As Christians, they exist in the corporate life of the whole Church, of which this or that "community" is the local representative.

[4] "St. Luke's narrative," says Bishop Lightfoot,

the "'Apostolate," as "unquestioned" and "supreme," forms "the basis and *background* of everything."[1] Apostles prescribe for the nascent Church its terms of communion; all contributions are laid at their feet; their "coryphæus," as St. Peter has been not untruly called, overawes the whole Church by the judgment which he calls down upon two offenders; even in what might seem a matter of "charity organisation," they bid the multitude choose seven men signally qualified, but reserve to themselves, as of

"represents the twelve Apostles in the earliest days as the *sole directors* and administrators of the Church" (Dissert. on Apost. Age, p. 144); "first of all, the Apostles themselves exercising the superintendence of all the churches under their care," etc. (ib. p. 157). The bishop, then, would hardly have approved of such a dictum as that "in the apostolic age, the *Ecclesia* itself," *i.e.* apparently the sum of all its male adult members, is . . . it would seem, even the primary authority" (Hort, p. 229); or that the expectation of Christ's speedy return would make "a governmental commission" an "anachronism" (Contemporary Review for August, 1898,—a signed article by a Congregationalist and an Anglican).

[1] Ministerial Priesthood, pp. 135, 145, 167.

course, the "appointment;"[1] in short, they take a line which can only explain itself in the light of a commission of authority from Him who had "all authority in heaven and on earth;" and certainly there is not a scrap of anything like evidence that they had accepted a commission from the Christian community.[2] But this, as we all know, is

[1] The force of Acts vi. 3, 6, is hardly given in Dr. Hort's statement (p. 100) that the "appointment was *sealed*, so to speak, by the Apostles praying and laying hands of blessing on the Seven." It was simply *made* by their act. Bishop Lightfoot is quite explicit on this point: "The persons were chosen by popular election, and *afterwards ordained by the Twelve* with imposition of hands" (Dissertations, p. 144). The two Contemporary Reviewers reduce this act to a mere "invocation of blessing." But this is to explain away καταστήσομεν. The fact that the Seven were already "full of the Spirit," so as to be endued with moral qualifications for appointment, cannot be held to abate the significance of that verb. Again, they refer to 1 Tim. iii. 10, as "suggesting that the *dokimasia* of the candidate was the most vital part of appointment." This is to confound the act with its prerequisite: and the text must be combined with 1 Tim. v. 22 (probably), 2 Tim. ii. 2, and Tit. i. 5.

[2] "Clavium potestas ... *nec in apostolos ab ecclesia*, sed in ecclesiam ab apostolis fuit derivata" (Bilson, De Perp. Eccl. Gub. p. 150. Bilson wrote in 1593).

not all. The martyrdom of the chief of the Seven was followed at no long interval by the conversion of one who "had been approving of his death," "who had not been with Our Lord during His stay upon earth, who was expressly a witness of that state of glory in which we believe that Christ is *now*,"[1] and who distinctly tells us that he was made an Apostle, "not from men, neither through man, but through Jesus Christ."[2]

---

[1] F. D. Maurice, Kingdom of Christ, ii. 188. St. Paul, we see, did not fulfil the condition referred to in Acts i. 21.

[2] St. Paul, then, was not made an Apostle by the mission recorded in Acts xiii. 3. But the imposition of hands is thrice ascribed by Dr. Hort to the Antiochene Christians as a body, or to their "representatives, official or other," on the ground that the "Divine command" would not be both conveyed and "executed" by the same persons (Hort, pp. 64, 216, 227). But the prophets and teachers might receive it as addressed to them, and then proceed to execute it; and the grammar of the passage decidedly suggests that this was so. Dr. Hort renders Acts xiv. 23, "having *chosen* for them elders" (p. 65); but a choice thus made by Paul and Barnabas alone would be in effect an appointment. This appointment was most likely a following of precedents set by senior Apostles at Jerusalem. Cp. R.V.

Here, then, is a new apostleship, created by what Dr. Hort truly calls a "direct commission," and in complete independence of the whole Christian body; and he who holds it not only ignores any apostleship as residing in that body, but takes especial care to show that he is not amenable to any "man's judgment."[1] In virtue of it, he issues commands, he exercises jurisdiction, even when absent, in the affairs of a local Church, and he everywhere bears himself as Christ's legate, endued with the amplest power.[2] Did he, then, as an Apostle, hold a more direct and real commission from Christ than did St. Peter or St. John? Assuredly his own assertion of full apostolic rights, in

---

[1] 1 Cor. iv. 3; 2 Cor. xii. 19; Gal. i. 10. He is not, *quâ* Apostle, the servant of the congregation. He "*brought himself*," indeed, "under bondage to all, that he might gain the more," and "proclaimed himself to be a bondservant" of the Corinthians "for Jesus' sake;" but this was in self-abnegation for the purposes of his own work, for the service of the common Master.

[2] Bishop Bilson, De Perp. Eccl. Gub. p. 82.

reply to the Judaizers' challenge, is a proof that the "very chiefest Apostles," whom he affirms to be in no sort his superiors,[1] had exercised the same "authority which the Lord had given him for building up, and not for casting down;" even as the last survivor of the Twelve declared himself resolved to exert it in correction of conduct which seems to have been virtual rebellion.[2]

Then, as to St. James the Just, Dr. Hort considers[3] that he was "taken up into the place among the Twelve vacated by" the martyrdom of "his namesake." This involves the opinion now widely held, but

---

[1] By way of proving that the Apostles had only "a claim to deference," as distinct from "a right to be obeyed," Dr. Hort (p. 84) refers to Gal. ii. 6. St. Paul, however, is not there speaking as a private Christian, but as an Apostle on an equal footing with the "pillars."

[2] 3 John 10. If the position of Diotrephes was "prelatic," he, like too many others in Church history, made his official authority to subserve a personal love of rule. Perhaps he persuaded himself that St. John, in old age, had become too "easy-going."

[3] Cp. Hort, pp. 77-79, 105.

anyhow not beyond question, that he was not "James the son of Alphæus;" but, waiving that point, one observes that, according to Dr. Hort, he was invested—apparently by the Twelve—with a "recognised office or function," not only of "authority," but of "government," over the local Church of Jerusalem—with "a definite charge," which "would of necessity become more distinct and, so to speak, *monarchical*, when the other Apostles were absent."[1] That they, having by hypothesis no "commission of government" from Christ, should take on themselves to make a new Apostle, and set him to "govern" the parent Church, has at least an appearance of inconsistency.

On the whole, then, we may say that the New Testament, naturally interpreted, supports the belief that Christ did will to

---

[1] On ἐγὼ κρίνω, in Acts xv. 19, Dr. Hort seems clearly right in saying that the sense is, "I, for my part, judge;" "This is my vote," as we should say.

found a perpetual ministry, and that He did commit its functions in their fulness to "the glorious company" of the selected Twelve.

(3.)

But it gradually became manifest that the "age" of the Gospel would not be so speedily "consummated" as at first it was natural to expect. In the second of St. Paul's extant letters, he has to warn some impulsive minds that much had to happen before the day of the Lord should come. Year by year it would become more probable, more evident, that provision must be made for a post-apostolic period. Of the two Pauline passages[1] which enumerate classes of persons specially "set by God in the Church," or "given by Christ to the Church," and in both of which "prophets," as representing one effect of the Pentecostal effusion, are ranked next after apostles; the second,

---

[1] 1 Cor. xii. 28; Eph. iv. 11.

which belongs to the first Roman imprisonment, places "evangelists," or missionaries, after prophets, and then puts together "pastors and teachers." These, like those who "presided over" the Church of Thessalonica,[1] or those who, as "having the rule," were to be "obeyed" with "submission" by the Hebrews,[2] may be identified with the

---

[1] Dr. Hort admits (p. 126) that the persons described as προϊσταμένους ὑμῶν ἐν Κυρίῳ in 1 Thess. v. 12 "are to all appearance office-bearers." Yet he seems anxious to minimise their official character. The participle, he observes, "is usually applied to informal leaderships and managings of all kinds, rather than to definite offices;" but is there a more natural process than that an informal term should come to be used formally? He adds that *all* the Thessalonians are exhorted to "admonish the disorderly;" but would not the duty of "guiding in the Lord" (as he renders it; but cp. 1 Tim. iii. 4) give a special character to the "guides'" admonition? The Contemporary Reviewers seem to think that St. Paul's exhortation in 1 Cor. xvi. 16, as to the due recognition of "volunteer" Church workers, tells against any authorised ministry. But the "highest" estimate of such a ministry is consistent with deferential regard for spiritual aptitudes and activities in laymen.

[2] Heb. xiii. 7, 17. The function designated in ἡγουμένων, ἡγουμένοις (cp. Acts xv. 22, on Judas and Silas), must be

presbyters whom we have heard of as ministering in Palestine and in the south-east of Asia Minor. Their title was borrowed from the synagogue, but received a new significance in the Church,[1] for they had definitely sacred functions, as of bearing spiritual rule, of praying over the sick, and therefore, probably, of leading the common worship; and although all of them did not actually teach, yet the more a presbyter "laboured in teaching," the nearer did he come up to his official standard. They were, we may be sure, the same who are called, —whether as a regular "title," or by a phrase "descriptive of function"[2]—*episkopoi*,

that of an *official* "leadership," involving the duty of teaching; and it had existed long enough to have been held by some who had passed away.

[1] As Dr. Hort well says (p. 101), "The unique redemption to which the *Ecclesia* owed its existence involved . . . the filling out what might have been mere administration with spiritual aims and forces."

[2] Dr. Hort takes the latter view (pp. 99, 190, 212): yet in p. 211 he assumes ἐπισκοπή to be an "office."

overseers or superintendents,—a name linked with "holding to the word that is trustworthy according to the teaching,"[1] with "taking charge of the flock," with acting as "stewards" in God's household. Were such officers, then, to be the supreme functionaries in the Church of the future? Did the Apostles indicate that such rule as they themselves had exercised was to be thereafter held by presbyteral colleges? We know much more of St. Paul's proceedings than of any other Apostle's; we know, for instance, that on his way to Palestine at the end of

---

He says that "if ἐπίσκοπον" in Tit. i. 7 "is a title of office, the article before it is without motive;" but see Bishop Ellicott *in loc.* and on Gal. iii. 20, that the article thus used represents "the generic idea," as we might say, of any ἐπίσκοπος, an ἐπίσκοπος as such. "The Apostle changes the former designation into the one that presents the subject most clearly in his *official* capacity." And when Dr. Hort suggests that St. Paul, in Phil. i. 1, "is *probably thinking less of the men* coming under either head" (*i.e.* ἐπισκόποις καὶ διακόνοις) "than of the *Ecclesia* as a whole" (p. 212), is not this somewhat arbitrary?

[1] Tit. i. 9; 1 Pet. v. 2; Tit. i. 7.

the third missionary journey, he had left the important Church of Ephesus in the charge of presbyters, whom he had solemnly addressed as "overseers appointed by the Holy Spirit to tend the Church of God."[1] This adds significance to the fact that, some eight years later, he commissioned a man still comparatively young, a native of a

---

[1] Acts xx. 28. Perhaps the most curious instance of Dr. Hort's bias against the idea of ministerial intervention is his suggestion that this appointment was probably made by the Ephesian *Ecclesia* itself, *because* "the Holy Spirit is elsewhere associated with joint acts, acts involving fellowship" (p. 100). Surely the Holy Spirit is not bound to a plurality of instruments; and the fact that Peter and John acted together in confirming (as we should say) the Samaritan converts was not understood at the time to imply that neither could have so acted by himself (Acts viii. 19). It was after Peter alone had spoken that the Holy Spirit "fell" on his hearers at Cæsarea (Acts x. 44). It was when Paul alone had laid his hands on certain disciples at Ephesus that the Holy Spirit came on them (Acts xix. 6). Another instance of this peculiarity occurs at p. 162, where "unto a work of ministration" (Eph. iv. 12) is thus glossed: "these more conspicuous functions were meant to train and develop analogous functions of ministration in *each and all*" (but cp. Eph. iii. 7).

distant province, to represent him in the supreme government of this Church of Ephesus, and invested him, not only with power to ordain, but with full disciplinary authority even over presbyters, equivalent to that which he entrusted to Titus in Crete,[1] although with a charge to require full evidence before taking any judicial action.[2] And when he knew that his own

---

[1] Tit. ii. 15: "with all authority to *command*." Dr. Mason well observes: "In the directions which the Pastoral Epistles give for the ordination of elders, no hint is conveyed that elders can be made by the Christian communities themselves. Their appointment is seen to rest wholly with a Timothy or a Titus, who has received plenary authority for the purpose from the Apostle himself" (Princ. of Eccl. Unity, p. 93. Cp. above, p. 21).

[2] The distinction between "with" and "through" in 1 Tim. iv. 11, 2 Tim. i. 6, is inadequately recognised by Dr. Hort, who supposes that St. Paul's part in the transaction (which he assumes to have been exceptional) was simply that of adding his own "blessing," as "Timothy's father in the faith" (p. 187). Nor does "the context" of 2 Tim. i. 6 "exclude the thought of a χάρισμα meant specially for Ephesian administration or teaching." On the contrary, this is just what St. Paul has in mind up to

course was nearly over,—or, as he himself puts it, that "the time of his departure was come,"—did he simply recall his deputy, and replace the administration in the hands of the presbytery? This would have been the natural, one might even say the necessary course, if a presbyterian polity had been in his mind for the future. But in his very last letter he does the exact opposite. Timothy, to be sure, is earnestly requested to visit him in his Roman prison before winter. But he is yet more earnestly charged to "fulfil his ministry" *because* Paul himself is "on the point of being offered;"[1] so that, when bereft of his principal, he is to assume the position of a chief pastor with intrinsic authority,

---

[2] Tim. ii. 2, and afterwards. And if the χάρισμα given to Timothy "was a special fitness bestowed by God to enable Timothy to fulfil a distinctive function" (p. 185), would not the "kindling up" of it (not necessarily "*re-*kindling," cp. Bishop Ellicott, *in loc.*) have a reference to the enlargement and elevation of Timothy's "function" as ruler of the church at Ephesus?

[1] 2 Tim. iv. 5, 6.

and is warned that a time not yet come, but coming, will task all his energies in an increasingly arduous work. This is somewhat like transforming an Apostle's vicar into an Apostle's successor;[1] and it may illustrate one form of the development of the ministry into the system with which we are familiar.[2] But other modes would prevail in other circumstances. Here a leading and specially

[1] Cp. Hooker, E.P. vii. 4. 2, and Shirley on The Apostolic Age, p. 117.
[2] Bilson observes that such a charge could only be entrusted to men "quorum fidem, gravitatem, et prudentiam, perinde atque ingenium et doctrinam, perspectam haberent Apostoli;" and such men were not to be found "at once everywhere" in an age when St. Paul could write as he does in Phil. ii. 20 (De Perp. Eccl. Gub. pp. 271, 275). Cp. Duchesne, Origines du Culte, Chr. p. 8, that the local presbyters "recognised the authority of Apostles of divers orders, founders and spiritual teachers," and "à mesure que disparaissent ces grands chefs, on voit apparaître la hiérarchie définitive" of "évêque en chef,"—"autour de lui, et formant collège avec lui, le conseil des prêtres—au-dessous, les diacres." He adds that, although "la communauté désignait ordinairement les personnes," "cette hiérarchie tenait ses pouvoirs, directement ou indirectement, des apôtres eux-mêmes."

energetic presbyter might be set over his brethren; there an active missionary or "evangelist," who previously had gone his rounds through a wide district, would be settled in the fulness of his experience as a single chief minister at its centre;[1] and although the gift of "prophecy," as described, for instance, in 1 Cor. xiv., seems to stand apart from administrative qualifications, and from the status of an "order,"[2] yet one who

---

[1] See an able article in the Church Quarterly Review for April 1887, which shows how events at the close of the apostolic period, tending to consolidate the churches of central towns, would thereby tend to merge the itinerant ministry in the stationary. In 2 Tim. iv. 5, the term "evangelist" seems to have lost something of its missionary significance; and in Acts xxi. 8, it is applied to Philip as ordinarily resident in the capital of Palestine.

[2] Cp. Moberly, Ministerial Priesthood, p. 166. Too much has been made of "The Teaching of the Apostles," as evidential in regard to sub-apostolic Church life. It issues, so to speak, from a corner; it is narrowly Judæo-Christian, not positively Ebionitic, but quite below the apostolic standard of Christianity. What it says of "apostles," *i.e.* itinerant missionaries, and of "prophets," also itinerant, both classes being distinct from the local

possessed it might also, like Polycarp, exhibit a special aptitude for spiritual "rule." It is difficult to fix the date of the Apocalypse: but those "angels" of the Churches who are there addressed as morally answerable for the condition of their Churches may be most naturally understood as holding a position equivalent to that which we now call episcopal—by whatever name it may then have been described.[1] St. John is thought to have

ministry, can hardly be taken as representing a general fact. On its general character, cp. Salmon, Non-canonical Books, p. 54 ff.; Gore on The Ministry, p. 412 ff.

[1] Prof. Ramsay's view, that the "angel" was "a permanent *episkopos*, yet had no authority *ex officio*" (The Church in the Roman Empire, p. 368), seems inconsistent with language in which the angel is treated as open to censure for neglect. One seems to see that he has a disciplinary function, in the discharge of which he must not be lax; and this *is* "authority *ex officio*." Such an *onus* of responsibility excludes the "guardian angel" theory. And the theory of "personified characteristics" for good and evil will not suit the description of all the "angels," including those of Laodicea and Sardis, as stars in the Son of Man's right hand; not to say that "angel" is a descriptive term, not a symbolic. And as for the transition, partial or complete,

"matured" or organised episcopacy in the west of Asia Minor; it has even been said that its institution "cannot be dissevered from his name without violence to historical testimony;"[1] and he would remember the

from "thou" to "you" in two of the letters (Rev. ii. 10, 24), Ignatius, writing to Polycarp, passes abruptly from singular to plural in c. 6, and back again in c. 7.

[1] *I.e.* that of the Muratorian Fragment, Clement of Alexandria (Quis Dives, 42), Tertullian (adv. Marc. iv. 5), and "other more direct evidence," cp. Lightfoot's Dissertations, pp. 172, 198. He speaks of this episcopacy as "firmly and widely" (though not universally) "established" at the end of "the last three decades of the first century, and, consequently, during the lifetime of the latest surviving Apostle" (ib. p. 160). In another passage the like is said as to "Apostle*s*, more especially St. John," and with reference to "the regions where" they "fixed *their* abode," and to "a time when its prevalence cannot be dissociated from *their* influence or *their* sanction" (p. 191; cp. Iren. iii. 3. 4, as to Polycarp). If this does not amount to an "apostolic institution of episcopacy," words have no meaning. It is true that Lightfoot speaks of "the power of the office" as "developed during the second and third centuries;" but he admits that this development was "providential" (p. 198), and, in an earlier passage, he even says that in "half a century after the fall of Jerusalem, episcopacy was matured, and the Catholic Church consolidated" (p. 167). All these

place which "James the Lord's brother" had come to hold as resident head of the Church of Jerusalem. These indications throw light upon, and are themselves reinforced by, the words of Clement of Rome[1] at the end of the first century, to the effect that the Apostles, in view of their own departure, had given "an additional direction"[2]

passages are in his Essay on the Ministry. In his SS. Ignatius and Polycarp (i. 377), the "development of a localised episcopate" is assigned to "the later years of the apostolic age;" and see other statements on the connection of episcopacy with the Apostles, collected in Dissertations (p. 241 ff.). His memory has sustained great injustice from one-sided quotation.

[1] In his Essay on the Ministry, Bishop Lightfoot calls Clement "rather the chief of the presbyters than the chief over the presbyters" (Dissert. p. 184); but in his St. Clement (i. 69, 81), "the chief ruler of the Roman church," who had "succeeded" Anencletus in its "government." The presbyters were, naturally enough, a great power in the most important of churches long after Clement's time; and if the episcopate did not, in those early days, stand out so prominently at Rome as it did a few years later at Antioch, this may have been due to some peculiar difficulties in unifying the Jewish and Gentile elements in the Roman church.

[2] See Lightfoot's note on Ignat. Trall. 7, "the

for the continuance of the ministry, by virtue of which, when those whom they had appointed as *episkopoi* (or presbyters) had fallen asleep,[1] "other approved men should succeed to their ministry," who, it appears from the context, were to be appointed by "men of repute."[2] These latter would be, for this purpose at any rate, successors of the

ordinances of the Apostles." One suggested reading, ἐπινομίν, in Clem. Cor. 44, is supported by a recently discovered and very ancient Latin version, which has "*postmodum legem dederunt*" (Mason, Princ. of Eccl. Unity, p. 98). Lightfoot thought it improbable; but it seems to be just the one variant which makes "have given" read naturally. (Cp. John i. 18, on the law as "given.") But whatever reading we adopt, the general purport is the same. Clement says that the *Apostles* made the necessary arrangement for the perpetuation of the ministry.

[1] This seems the natural construction of ἐὰν κοιμηθῶσιν.

[2] This is Lightfoot's rendering of ἐλλογίμων (cp. Clem. Cor. 44; cp. ib. 57, 62). The idea is not merely of reputation or esteem in man's judgment, but of Divine approval. Lightfoot assumes that the ἐλλόγιμοι belonged to the class of "approved men" above: if so, some of that class would appoint their own successors. But see Gore on the Ministry, p. 318. The sentence is badly

Apostles—acting, however, in regard to such ordinations, "with the approval of the whole Church;" they were to do, in this respect, exactly what Timothy and Titus had been commissioned by St. Paul to do at Ephesus and in Crete.[1] The *hegoumenoi* or *prohegoumenoi* whom Clement had already mentioned were apparently presbyters;[2] but it is anyhow clear that he assumes the principle of ministerial *succession;* the notion of a ministry appointed by the Christian community itself, a ministry "democratic" in basis, does not cross

written, but Clement's meaning seems clear. He does not suppose the Apostles to be alive (except in some cases) at the death of the earliest ministers; he says that they had previously provided for that event, and the provision consisted in this, that "other men of repute" should appoint the next generation of ministers.

[1] The Contemporary Reviewers regard them as "simply leading men of the community," employed by it to "install its elect." But this (1) ignores the collocation of the persons in question, as ordainers, with the Apostles; and (2) brings in the idea of congregational appointment, which is alien to the whole passage.

[2] Clem. Cor. 1, 21.

his mind.[1] But if that community, being immortal as such, had indeed been collectively invested with apostleship, it is not conceivable that its function of creating ministerial offices, and filling them up when vacated, could so soon have become obsolete. We are here looking into what Dr. Salmon has called the "tunnel" of sub-apostolic history: it is a time of transition, and dim for want of sufficient documentary evidence; but some ten years after St. John's death bring us to the last days of the life of Ignatius, and then the "three orders" of bishop, presbyter, and

---

[1] Hermas, writing in reference to the Roman church (he mentions Clement) professes to convey warnings τοῖς προηγουμένοις τῆς ἐκκλησίας καὶ τοῖς πρωτοκαθεδρίταις (Vis. iii. 9. 7). Grammatically this would suggest two classes, but Hermas probably had in mind only one—that of presbyters, whom elsewhere he calls προϊσταμένων (Vis. ii. 4, 3). But in Vis. iii. 5. 1, he speaks of "apostles, and bishops, and teachers, and deacons," thus distinguishing "bishops" as a second class from "teachers" as a third; and by "teachers" we naturally understand presbyters. His date is still somewhat dubious, but Salmon places him *early* in the second century (Non-canonical Books,

deacon appear as in possession, speaking generally, of the Asiatic Churches, so that a bishop of the great Eastern capital, the birthplace of the Christian name, could affirm that "apart from them, one does not speak of a Church."[1] Ignatius, to be sure, says

---

p. 24). Dorner takes the usually received date (middle of second century), and thinks that Hermas, in his dread of formality as connected with ecclesiastical officialism, anticipated the Montanist point of view.

[1] Trall. 3. The two Contemporary Reviewers affirm that the Ignatian bishop is "undoubtedly the single bishop, *or congregational pastor*, in the sense common to most modern churches." Has the "modern congregational pastor" a council of presbyters and a body of clerical or ministerial deacons under him? On the Ignatian letters, as indicating "the immense impulse which somehow rooted and grounded firmly throughout the whole Church . . . that episcopal system which constituted the apostolic unity of government," cp. H. S. Holland, The Apostolic Fathers, p. 141. Grant that the process was gradual; still, if its result was to destroy a pre-existing system of "presbyterian parity," it would surely have provoked first suspicion and then resistance, and some evidence of a struggle would remain. But Irenæus, writing about sixty years after the death of Ignatius, "betrays no knowledge of a time when episcopacy was not" (Dissert. p. 190), and traces it unhesitatingly to apostolic institution. Other matters were "eagerly canvassed"

nothing in his letter to the Romans about their bishop, but neither does he say anything about their ministers; and he assumes that the episcopate is an institution which they themselves will understand and respect.[1]

(ib.); in particular, a difference about the time of observing a great annual festival very nearly produced a schism; but the typical theologian of his time, the pupil of Polycarp, who held in his hands such various threads of tradition, who had lectured at Rome (perhaps while Hegesippus was drawing up his list of its bishops), is as clear about episcopacy as about the faith or the Gospels. Tertullian, as a Catholic, is equally distinct; and even the Alexandrian Clement, in a context full of his peculiar idealism, describes "the grades of bishops, presbyters, and deacons" as earthly counterparts of "angelic glory;" and it is implied that the episcopate represents the apostolate (Strom. vi. 107). (Cp. Pæd. iii. 97, where he assumes that ἐπίσκοπος in the New Testament means a bishop.) This is fuller and therefore more suggestive language than that in Strom. vii. 3, where presbyters are said to represent the idea of improvement (in the condition of the Church), and deacons that of attendance (ὑπηρετικήν). Here Clement is referring to work of a kind in which bishops and presbyters substantially co-operate.

[1] Rom. c. 2, "the bishop of Syria;" still more, ib. 9, "Jesus Christ alone, and your love, will act as bishop of

Settlement of Episcopacy gradual. 43

No one now supposes that the settlement of episcopacy was the affair of a year, or

the church in Syria" (*i.e.* until my successor can be appointed). It is true that Ignatius does not describe bishops as representatives of Apostles; but he does what is more, he describes them as representing the highest spiritual authority, that of "the Father" in His relation to Christ (Magn. 3, 6, 13; Trall. 3; Smyrn. 8); or of Christ either in His relation to His Apostles, or absolutely (Eph. 6; Trall. 2): and this explains the comparison of the presbyters to the Apostles (Magn. 6; Trall. 2, 3; Smyrn. 8), and what Lightfoot calls the "startling comparison of the deacon to Jesus Christ" (as doing the Father's will in His earthly ministry: Trall. 3). To have written thus of a merely local or experimental polity would have been the very extravagance of assumption. His language is doubtless balanced by pointed references to the dignity of the presbyteral council; but it is quite inconsistent with the idea of a mere episcopal "chairmanship." He does not refer to the bishop as a judge of his presbyters; but it would not have suited his purpose to dwell on such faults in the second order of the threefold ministry as might require the exercise of superior jurisdiction. As to Philippi, Dr. Moberly has laid stress on the quasi-episcopal tone of St. Polycarp's letter as unnatural if he were addressing a church with a "presbyteral constitution," but very intelligible if the Philippians were just then without a chief pastor (Minist. Priesthood, p. 203). The Contemporary Reviewers profess to "brush this aside by one solid analogy"—that of the letters of Dionysius of Corinth to churches which had

was effected everywhere under the same conditions and at the same rate. Rather was the mode of it various: it came on earlier here, somewhat later there,[1] and surely it is significant that it appeared "more rapidly in Jerusalem and Antioch and Ephesus," *i.e.* in the older seats of Christianity, than "where the influences were more purely Greek."[2] Again, the "prelates" set over Churches would not always have precisely the same powers, any more than precisely the same tasks: and, generally, the dignity of presbyters under

---

bishops. The analogy is hardly "solid." Dionysius writes on topics of general church interest or current controversy; Polycarp's letter is like a pastoral.

[1] Epiphanius says rather quaintly, "Everything had not all things from the very first, but as time went on τὰ πρὸς τελείωσιν τῶν χρειῶν κατηρτίζετο" (Hær. 75. 5).

[2] Cp. Lightfoot, Dissertations, p. 190. Observe that one church which did not possess it when Clement of Rome wrote was that same Corinthian community which had given so much trouble to St. Paul himself by its party divisions and its insubordination. It is quite natural that when Corinthians were to be admonished, the admonition should come explicitly from the great Roman church, not from the bishop in his own person.

episcopal pre-eminence is illustrated by the term "presbyter" repeatedly applied, as by St. Irenæus, to bishops, apparently as embodying a trustworthy tradition, and so linking the present to the past;[1] or by the

[1] In iii. 2. 2, Irenæus uses the term presbyters for bishops, including living bishops, as guardians of tradition; so, too, in iv. 26. 2, 4, 5. In two passages quoted by Eusebius (v. 20, 24), he applies it, with the same intention, to deceased bishops, one of them being Polycarp. In other passages he uses the title for those who had heard from hearers of Apostles. Papias applies it vaguely both to Apostles and their hearers (see Lightfoot, Supernat. Religion, p. 145). Clement of Alexandria, in the story of the young robber, uses bishops in the ordinary sense as distinct from clergy, but also calls the person to whom St. John entrusts the young man both "bishop," πρεσβύτερος, and πρεσβύτης. Hippolytus (?), in the "Refutation," calls his own teacher Irenæus "the blessed presbyter;" the *seniores* whom Tertullian describes as "presiding" are probably bishops; and Döllinger considers that Firmilian, in his letter to Cyprian, uses "elders" both for bishops specially qualified as "holders of Church traditions" and for all bishops in general (Hipp. Kall. p. 341). After all, bishops might be called presbyters if St. Peter himself assumed the name (1 Pet. v. 1); and all "episcopalians" admit that the two "orders" have functions in common. But if a bishop was sometimes in this period called a presbyter, was a presbyter ever called a bishop?

similarity in some very ancient Roman canons of the forms of ordination for bishops and for presbyters.[1] Some time in any case

---

[1] The so-called "Hippolytean" canons are supposed by Batiffol to belong to the Roman church about 195 (Anc. Littér. Chrét. Gr. p. 159). They prescribe that when a bishop is to be ordained, "one from among the bishops and presbyters" shall lay his hand on his head and say the prayer. The writer here seems to regard the bishops and presbyters assembled as forming one group; but the one person coming forward out of it must be presumed to be a bishop, for we afterwards read, "the power of ordaining is not given to a presbyter" (Can. Hipp. ed. Achelis, p. 62). The last words are like a question asked by Jerome: "What does a bishop do that a presbyter does not, except ordaining?" (Ep. 146). This may show that when, just before, he asserts that up to the time of bishops Heraclas and Dionysius, of whom the former became bishop in 231, the Alexandrian presbyters "chose one of their own number and named him bishop, just as if an army were making an imperator, or deacons nominating an archdeacon," he does not suppose that the consecration of such a bishop was performed by presbyteral hands. Indeed, his two illustrations imply the intervention of a superior authority; for the army's choice had constitutionally to be ratified by the authoritative act of the senate, and Bingham says (ii. 21. 2), that any electoral power in the deacons must be understood to be under the direction of the bishop, to whom the archdeacon stood in a specially confidential relation. In

would be required for the institution to take its mould; and we may call the process, if we please, a "development," which is but another word for an "evolution," although this latter term, as commonly used, may seem rather more ambiguous. Anyhow, the fact that, even before the last Apostle's departure, such different lines of Church life, and Church action converged towards episcopacy, is a token that the movement towards this one goal was the result of a "vital energy"[1]

this same letter Jerome says that "all bishops are successors of the Apostles." On his statements, and on that of Eutychius, an Egyptian patriarch of the tenth century, who makes some strange blunders about the early Church history of Egypt, see Bishop Charles Wordsworth's Outlines of the Christian Ministry, pp. 164-187, 197-203, and Prof. Mason, Princ. of Eccles. Unity, p. 96. *Consignant*, in Pseudo-Ambrose, refers to confirmation, not to ordination; so Innocent I. Ep. 1. 3: and "even if *consecrant* is the correct reading, it must mean the consecration of the chrism "applied" after baptism (Mason, l.c.). So in Qu. Vet. Nov. Test. 101.

[1] Cp. Fr. Benson, Introd. to Exp. of Ep. to Romans, p. x. "God's vital energy," he says, "worked with the various communities of the growing Christendom in

in a divinely-guided Church, the inevitable expansion of a germ inherent in apostolic Christianity, and, above all, the expression of an original purpose of Christ. We have His recorded acts and words at the beginning of a period, and the Ignatian evidence at its close; and this warrants us in supposing that, during the obscurer sub-apostolic part of that period, events were being disposed towards that result, as contemplated by the will of Him who had said that He would place stewards over His household,[1] who

---

various ways while the organism was forming, but everywhere the law of vital growth was leading to the same result."

[1] Cp. p. 15. Cyprian alludes to this in Ep. 59. 5; "*sacerdotes*, id est, *dispensatores* ejus" (Dei). The question of "priesthood" will come again before us; but it may here be observed that a man's view as to the origin of the ministry will be found to run up (as it were) into his view as to "means of grace." Cp. Gladstone, Church Principles, etc., pp. 192, 198, 220, 278. Of grace he says, "This gem, destined for an earthly use, requires a casket" [at any rate, a casket has been provided], "this casket a keeper." If Luke xii. 42 were a newly discovered text, claiming to be part of a Gospel, not a few would

sent forth the first holders of that trust as He had been sent by the Father, and who probably reject it at once, as "condemned by its sacerdotalism."

But let that pass. The Contemporary Reviewers observe that "there are really only two theories of order" (*i.e.* of ordination) "that need serious consideration:" one, that which "makes valid ministry depend on appointment by the Christian society, more or less localised;" the other, that of succession or transmission. Dr. Liddon had said just the same in a remarkable consecration sermon ("A Father in God," in Clerical Life and Work, p. 292); but he took care to describe the latter theory (which the Reviewers call "high-clerical" rather than "high-church") as "tracing ministerial authority to the person of Our Lord, who deposited it . . . in the college of the Apostles." On the other theory, indeed, the question of validity could hardly come up; for the newest and smallest group or subsection of Christians might claim to be an adequate local representation of "the Christian society" for the purpose of appointing ministers, who would be, in fact, simply its own committeemen; and, on that showing, any one ministry would be just as "valid" as another. But when Churchmen are summoned to accept a theory which involves a reversal of their idea of ministry and Church, they may fairly demand real evidence that it *is* the theory of the New Testament,—that it was taught, or assumed, or implied by the Apostolic writers,—that it was acted on by the contemporary "Christian society,"—and, one may add, that it was inherited by the sub-apostolic Church—to go no

thereby indicated that the future ministry must be somehow in true organic connexion with those on whom He had breathed.

further down. For example: do the earliest Christian documents encourage a consecrator or ordainer to say, as a Swedish archbishop has to say, in "committing the episcopal office" to a new bishop, that he acts by "authority entrusted to him, on God's behalf, *by the congregation*"? On this point our twenty-third Article, "vague" as it is, has a certain significance: it speaks of "authority to send ministers" as "given *in* the congregation," "*in* ecclesiâ." This leaves the Lutheran theory on one side, while the Ordinal implies the Catholic.

ADDRESS II.

(1.)

TWENTY years ago Mr. Gladstone expressed his belief that "the Church began with a clergy,—nay, began *in* a clergy,—had its centre of life and of self-propagating power in the Apostolic college, which gradually called into being those orders that form the full equipment of the Christian ministry," but that the principle of "hierarchy" which, left to itself, might have become "absolute," was "girt about on every side with limiting conditions," which secured the co-ordination of freedom with authority.[1] To say, then, as has been said, that the first Christian community was "not a *mere horde* of men ruled *absolutely* by the Apostles, but a true body

[1] Gladstone, Gleanings, iii. 262.

politic, in which different functions were assigned to different members, and a share of responsibility rested upon the members at large, each and all," [1]—is to contradict what nobody affirms, and to affirm what nobody contradicts. We all know what St. Paul says on the latter point; and as to the former, we have seen that officers whom we read of as appointed by Apostles, and as amenable to the jurisdiction even of apostolic delegates, were yet invested with some kind of "rule," so that, *à fortiori*, Apostles themselves were rulers in a fuller sense—but it was not the sense of despotism. They ruled paternally—one might even say, fraternally: they remembered that the Lord Himself had made them His "friends" and confidants, had even "been among them as he that serveth," and had forbidden them to imitate "the kings of the Gentiles."[2] The one

---

[1] Hort, The Christian Ecclesia, p. 52.
[2] "Quid mirum si apostolis a Christo sit interdictum

Apostle who held, in the earliest days at least, and to some extent in partnership with St. John, an acknowledged prominence or leadership, not only accepts the rebuke of a junior Apostle as in point of authority "no whit behind" himself,—not only exhorts Asiatic presbyters as if a "fellow-presbyter," and bids them "not to lord it over their portions of the flock,"—but meets a remonstrance from prejudiced Hebrew Christians by patiently narrating the circumstances which they had misunderstood. Or observe

ne regali aut herili jure in fratres dominentur, id est, ne tanquam servis imperent, aut eos cogant et puniant ut mancipia? ... Non tamen quisquam putet auctoritatem aut honorem pastoralem hac ratione labefactari aut imminui ... Pastores ... Christus non metui tanquam dominos, sed coli ac diligi tanquam parentes ... contra, pastores non dominari sed pascere, non terrere sed ducere ..., voluit. Quod siquid alicubi præcipiant, aut inobsequentes a cæteris summoveant, id in Christi nomine faciunt, ut illius voluntatis interpretes et mandatorum nuntii, qui solus in istiusmodi rebus imperandi jus habet; ipsi nihil aliud sunt quam conservi, aut ad summum œconomi," etc. (Bilson, De Perp. Eccl. Gub. p. 92).

St. Paul informing a Church, largely indocile and unduly self-complacent, that he "has already decided" to inflict punishment on a grievous offender by their collective voice in his own absence, but with his "presence in spirit,"[1] and then, in a second letter, on proof of repentance, promising to confirm, as "Christ's representative," the pardon which he directs them to bestow:[2] and in that same letter we find him threatening indeed on the one hand not to spare defiant sinners, but disclaiming "dominion over the faith of those" with whom his habitual *modestia apostolica* associates himself as "stablished in Christ." Or look to the conference or council described in the fifteenth chapter of Acts: a grave question, only too

---

[1] It is clear that he did not leave the Corinthians free to judge whether any punishment should be inflicted (see ἐγὼ . . . ἤδη κέκρικα . . . παραδοῦναι, 1 Cor. v. 3–5): as Bilson comments—"'Ego jam decrevi,' antequam ipse scriberet, antequam illi legerent" (De Perp. Eccl. Gub. p. 144). And cp. 2 Cor. ii. 10.

[2] It is not *they* who "forgive ἐν προσώπῳ Χριστοῦ."

likely to produce dissension, is referred to "the Apostles and presbyters" of the mother Church; they meet, but think it quite natural to admit the faithful of Jerusalem, at least in adequate numbers, to the discussion; and thus the assent of "the whole Church" is obtained for the "decrees" which are to be formulated,[1] although those decrees are afterwards distinctly declared to have been "ordained by the Apostles and presbyters," who, as Archbishop Potter puts it, "are described as principals in this whole affair,"[2] or, as Dr. Hort says, were understood to bear "the chief responsibility."[3]

[1] Irenæus notices this point: "Et universa ecclesia convenisset in unum" (iii. 12. 14).

[2] Church Government, p. 223.

[3] Hort, p. 70. Dr. Hort, adopting the Revised text of Acts xv. 23, "the apostles and the elder brethren," admits that "the *Ecclesia* is not separately mentioned in the salutation;" yet he pleads that the phrase used indicates that the presbyters "were *but* elder brothers at the head of a great family of brethren" (as if no "brother" could be superior to another in point of authority), and on that score thinks himself warranted

Even while conscious of specific authority, the pastors are minded, as we say, to carry the people with them, to address them as "wise men," to appeal, after the Master's own example,[1] to their moral reason, and thus, in the comprehensive Pauline phrase, to "commend themselves to every man's conscience in the sight of God."

Such is the Apostolic government—the very reverse of what has too often brought reproach on the very name of hierarchy, and which, in Our Lord's awful prophetic

---

in explaining "we," in the last clause of ver. 24, by "the apostles, elders, *and the whole Ecclesia*" (p. 68); which seems rather lax. He is also seriously inexact in his representation of ver. 22, "the apostles and the elders *and* all the *Ecclesia*" (p. 71). St. Luke wrote "*with* the whole ἐκκλησία"—a distinctive phrase, which clearly intimates that the part taken by the ἐκκλησία was that of concurrence in the resolutions of the Apostles and elders. In p. 82 Dr. Hort attenuates the force of τὰ δόγματα τὰ κεκριμένα, Acts xvi. 4. Surely Acts xv. 28 implies *not* "less than a command;" its form *is* "imperative."

[1] Luke xii. 57.

picture, appears side by side with sensual excess.[1] In that primeval Church there was "ample room and verge" for the voluntary personal element, for such individualism as was involved in the enhanced importance of every soul for which Christ had died, and which was meant to "grow up into Him in all things." There was no stiff, chilling, deadening exclusiveness—no mistrust of ministers by people, of people by ministers; the tide of mutual sympathy and confidence, of spontaneity in effort, of free-hearted contribution of "divers gifts" to the common cause,[2] was a river that made glad that rising city of God: the believers could habitually feel that those who in various degrees "had rule over them" were their own "brethren" and "fellow-servants," while "watching for their

---

[1] Matt. xxiv. 49; Luke xii. 45.
[2] This is a point which Dr. Hort repeatedly and most justly emphasises (pp. 15, 48, 123).

souls," and "guiding them in the Lord," and "praying that they might be perfected;" they had but little occasion to suspect their pastors of that terrible clerical fault, "the love of spiritual power" simply "*as* power:"[1] so that, if we may so express it, there could be no separation of interests between a community which Apostles, adopting the language of Exodus, had described as a "royal priesthood," and those who, having been specially made agents of the great High Priest, and officers under the invisible King, were thereby qualified to be the divinely provided representatives and organs of its corporate priestliness and royalty.[2]

[1] Cp. Liddon, Univ. Serm., ii. 201.

[2] In 1 Cor. iv. 1 the word rendered "ministers" is nowhere else used by St. Paul. But it is used of him in Acts xxvi. 16; and cp. Luke i. 2. He uses it here to describe himself as attending upon, and working under, Christ the Sovereign Agent. It is most important to observe that neither the priesthood of all baptised Christians, nor the priesthood of Christ, can be set

(2.)

And this leads us to consider a passage in

in opposition to a ministerial priesthood without a false antithesis. The former is exercised (1) in personal acts of approach to God in Christ, of self-dedication, or (2) in the common worship which culminates in the Eucharist; but when the individual comes within the sphere of churchly action, his priesthood is, as it were, enlarged into a participation in the "God-ward" priestly service of the whole body; and this, being corporate, requires an appointed organ to unify and set it in motion. That organ, in the Catholic conception, is found in the ministry, which is also Christ's instrument towards the Church, and which thus in both aspects of its work may be called "representative." See an admirable passage in Liddon's Univ. Serm. ii. 199, and another and longer context in Maurice's Kingdom of Christ, ii. 183 ff. Maurice contends that "every office in the Church is the image of some office performed by Christ in His own person, is the means by which that office is presented to men, and made effectual for them through all time." The minister's "whole object is to present Christ to men and men to Christ." When he is "in the congregation," he has "to represent its unity, to offer it before God as a whole body;" when he is "alone with any particular member of it, he has to preserve him in the unity of the Church, to present before God his" repentance. "But still, this can be but half his duty." There must be "a voice speaking from heaven as well as one crying from earth," etc. The term "representative," as applied

that "most effective"[1] letter of the Roman Church to the Corinthians, which is commonly and rightly called St. Clement's.[2] We

to the Christian ministry in its relation to the Church at large (as by Liddon, Gore, Moberly) is often misunderstood, on account of its association in matters political with the relation of a member of parliament to his constituents. But a "representative" is not necessarily a nominee. The eye "represents" the body in the exercise of the power of vision, but does not derive from the body its capacity for that function: it is an organ provided *for* the body. Cp. Bishop Moberly, quoted in Moberly's Minist. Priesthood, p. 70. Maurice, it may be added, applies the term "representative" to the *Jewish* high priest, as "consecrated to be a witness of the holiness of the congregation" (Kingdom of Christ, ii. 134).

[1] So Keble renders Irenæus's $ἱκανωτάτην$. Lightfoot renders it "most adequate." The idea is that it covers the whole ground, leaves nothing unsaid.

[2] In an essay on "The Position of the Laity in the Early Church," included in a volume of Essays on Church Reform, Mr. Rackham says that "St. Clement does not imply that, in the removal from their office of certain presbyters at Corinth, the laity had exceeded their powers, but that they had exercised them unjustly in removing ministers who were holy and blameless" (p. 36). "Removing," in such a case (as in others), is a somewhat euphemistic term; and one might ask how ministers described by Mr. Rackham as possessing "a commission from above" (p. 35) could be deprived of it by a deposition "from below." But does Clement "imply"

have already taken account of his words on
" the principle of ministerial" succession,

that the leaders of the Corinthian movement were acting within their constitutional rights, and that their fault was simply the misuse of lawful authority, such as we should discern in an oppressive act of parliament? What he says is, that they were seditious or factious, upsetters of order, men who "exalted themselves." He goes further yet, and warns them to remember the fate of Dathan and Abiram. And the whole drift of c. 40 ff. implies that to eject ministers was *not* within the functions of the laity. It is after he has enforced the duty of self-restriction within respective bounds that he adds the consideration of the personal merit of the sufferers. Nor does the language in c. 54 make it "evident that in matters of public importance the exercise of discipline rested with the whole body" (p. 37)—which, for the purpose of the argument, must mean that the people or laity had an acknowledged right to summon their ministers to resign office. What Clement contemplates is the case of a "high-minded" man, who, if his presence seems to be an occasion of strife, will say, "I retire whither you please; I do what is enjoined on me by the multitude." This is not ordinary obedience to regular authority, but an extraordinary self-sacrifice for the peace of the Church, such as the resignation of sees contemplated in a certain contingency by Catholic bishops in Africa (Aug. Ep. 128. 3). It is admitted that "at Corinth, for a time at least, the power of the people seems to have obtained an unduly predominant position" (p. 38). If so, they *did*, to some extent, "exceed their powers."

and the manner in which apostolic direction had set it to work; but some three chapters earlier we find him assuming a very real analogy between the Jewish and Christian systems in regard to the orderly distribution of official functions. He adduces the Old Testament regulations as to high priests, priests, and Levites, adding, "the layman is bound by what is prescribed to the laity." The titles are used primarily in their Jewish significance; but Clement is so full of the

Did they, or did they not? We must take this view or else that. And when one is told that in the Roman guilds of the period there was "a similar balance of authority" to that which existed in the Church—and that similarity is illustrated by the remark that in these societies, while the priests were independent in the performance of religious rites, "the constitution was *entirely democratic*," so that, "in the administration of business, all the power belonged to the assembly (consisting of all the members), its control was incessant, *its authority absolute*," and "the priests at the end of their term of office were accountable to it for the discharge of their functions" (p. 39)—one must ask whether it can be seriously maintained that a parallel state of things characterised the Church when apostleship was still fresh in the memory?

idea of a harmony combining the new order with the old, that he fuses together, in a manner almost perplexing, the indications of the Divine will in the past and in the present.[1] So that here, indirectly, we get the first use of "laic" for a member of that "whole body of the Church"[2] which St. Peter describes as "a chosen race, a holy nation, a people specially owned" by God, —the first use, that is, of a title of religious dignity, which to some extent even in England, and far more in France, has undergone of late years such an injurious desecration.[3] And we may infer from a later

[1] The language, to say the least, is "more natural if Clement had in view a threefold Christian ministry" (cp. Gore, The Ministry, p. 315). One thing is certain: he could not have written this c. 40 as it stands, if he had not believed the Christian ministry to have had just as Divine an origination as the Jewish.

[2] Second Collect for Good Friday.

[3] The frequent use of "lay" in antithesis to "ecclesiastical," or of "ecclesiastical" as equivalent to "clerical," is a stage in that process which results in the use of "laicised education" for education which systematically ignores God.

passage, that the function of "offering the gifts," or oblations, in a Christian sense,[1] belonging as it did to the presbyters whom Clement calls *episkopoi*, would not come within the line of "what was prescribed"

---

[1] After the fall of Jerusalem, "sacerdotal" language would become less liable to misconstruction. Accordingly, here it is used simply and, as it were, casually, by the earliest of the sub-apostolic fathers. Lightfoot, in one sentence, admits that "the Eucharistic elements" are included among the "gifts," although, in a summary further on in the same note, he omits all mention of them. But if they are oblations at all, they must, *being what they are*, have a unique place. And to say that, in Clement's view, "the minister is a priest in the same sense only in which each individual member of the congregation is a priest" (Dissert. p. 230), is surely to forget that the sacrificial service of the congregation, as representing the Church, is collective, and that its organ is therefore acting as no mere individual could act. The dread of "sacerdotalism" exhibited by Lightfoot's Essay on the Ministry may be not a little due to misconception (cp. Moberly, Minist. Priesthood, p. 76). But, anyhow, that essay appeared in 1868. Its author, speaking as a bishop to ordinands in 1881, asks, "What is your priesthood but the concentration of the priesthood of the whole people of Christ?" and in 1882 represents Our Lord as saying at the Judgment to one who has been His minister, "Answer this, thou priest of the Most High God" (Ordination Addresses, pp. 57, 78).

for Christian laics, although, of course, it was in close relation to the Church's corporate priesthood. A passage in St. Ignatius' letter to the Smyrnæans carries on the same thought. He does not expressly say that a layman may not celebrate the Eucharist, but he lays down a principle which would prevent any question of that kind from arising. After mentioning bishops, presbyters, and deacons, he says, "Let no man do anything pertaining to the Church apart from the bishop; let that Eucharist be deemed valid" (in the sense of proper or legitimate) "which is celebrated by" (literally, under), "the bishop, or by one whom he has commissioned" (for the purpose).[1] The close union of the presbyters with the bishop would exclude the notion of his commissioning any other to fulfil an office which was

[1] Smyrn. 8. Further on in the chapter he says, "It is not permissible either to baptise or to hold (lit. *make*) an Agape apart from the bishop." On the Agape, cp. below, p. 106.

ordinarily his.¹ Tertullian, writing before his secession, blames "heretics" for "imposing even on laymen the functions of priesthood;" and, even as a Montanist, affirms, "We take the Eucharist from no other hands than those of our presidents," meaning the bishops and presbyters.² But when in another Montanistic treatise, "An Exhortation to Chastity," he is contending that laymen are as much bound as priests to refrain from second marriages, he first of all cites Rev. i. 6, then says that "it is the Church's authority, and the dignity made sacred by the *consessus ordinis*," that is, by admission to a seat among the presbyters, "which constitutes³ the difference between

---

¹ Hence the specific use of the title *sacerdos* for a bishop.
² De Præscr. Hær. 41 ; De Cor. 3.
³ *Constituit* should be understood as in the present tense. The reference is to the rite of ordination. Tertullian could not mean that the ministry was only of ecclesiastical institution ; for in De Monogamia, 12, as in De Fuga, 13, he assumes it to be of apostolic origin, and takes notice of a frequent misuse of Rev. i. 6.

the ordained and the people," and proceeds, "Thus where is no such *consessus*" (*i.e.* where no presbyter is available), "you" (the ordinary lay Churchman), "both offer, and baptise, and are priest alone for yourself. But where there are three, though they be laics, there is a Church" (a favourite Montanistic formula).[1] His theory is that every layman has a potential "priestly right," which in ordinary circumstances will for order's sake lie dormant, but which a peculiar emergency can call into exercise. This can hardly be called a satisfactory exposition of

---

[1] Bp. Kaye marks it as suspicious in regard to the De Baptismo that the sixth chapter states (with a very bold adaptation) the "notion that three persons compose a Church, which frequently occurs in the works confessedly written after he became a believer in the New Prophecy" (Eccl. Hist. Illustrated from Tertullian, p. 48). Tertullian's notions of inference from a text are sometimes extraordinary. Here he goes on, "*For* every one 'lives by his own faith,' and 'there is no acceptance of persons with God,' for 'not the hearers of the law,'" etc. The dictum that three laics are a Church (a misrepresentation of Matt. xviii. 20) is in express opposition to Ignatius' statement in Trall. 3.

the language of St. John or St. Peter, which surely refers to something normal and permanently active;[1] but passing this by, can we take Tertullian's account of what takes place when clergy are not at hand as in fact representing a Churchly usage? It may be granted[2] that he *seems* to be giving it as such, and assuming that no Churchman can dispute it. But this does not count for so

[1] On this cp. Gladstone, Church Principles, etc., p. 269; Liddon, Univ. Serm. ii. 198 ff. It is a characteristic of false or corrupt sacerdotalism to suggest or support the notion that the clergy have to *do* the laymen's religion for them, or that the ordained man is, as such, *personally* nearer to God than the unordained. The absolute negation of this idea is one safeguard against *such* a sacerdotalism: and the principle that "grace is not tied to sacraments" is another. Cp. Gore, The Ministry, p. 84.

[2] Waterland, indeed, grants nothing of the sort, and says that Tertullian is here "drawing an inference from his former position," and "not speaking the sense of the Church" (Works, vi. 166). So Abp. Potter, Ch. Gov. p. 413; and so Döllinger (Hippol. und Kallist. p. 350), that he is not speaking "von einer in der Kirche bestehenden anerkannten Sitte," but merely stating a conclusion from his own theory of the spiritual or "higher" Church. Cp. also Moberly, Minist. Priesthood, p. 78.

much in his case as it might in another's; for the "fervid African," especially under what Hooker calls the "exulceration of mind" produced by his fierce sectarian partisanship, is perhaps the most reckless of all arguers, ancient or modern.[1] He would not think twice about inferring a custom from an isolated case,—itself, perhaps, resting on rumour; or about advancing from the known fact—supposing it to be a fact—of lay baptism in case of necessity,[2] to the assertion of a similar recognition of lay celebration, because, to his mind, the latter was involved

---

[1] Hooker, E.P. ii. 5. 7. So Archd. Evans, Biogr. of Early Church, i. 359: "His rashness often leads him into assertions which he cannot support. . . . Sometimes, sooner than say nothing in reply, he will almost say anything."

[2] It has, indeed, been disputed whether his words about laymen's exceptional right to baptise (De Bapt. 17) can be taken as based on Church practice. See Bingham on Lay Baptism, i. 1. 8, for the affirmative, and Waterland, vi. 163, for the negative. But cp. Euseb. vi. 5, where "the brethren" administer baptism to Basilides in prison during a persecution.

in the former. But it is clear that the ministrations in question do not lose, for him, aught of their "sacerdotal" character, if undertaken by unordained persons in virtue of a latent sacerdotal "right" which an emergency calls into exercise. He does not, so to speak, depress the priest to the level of the layman, but rather elevates the layman, for the time, to that of the priest.[1]

(3.)

Lay preaching was a different matter. In the apostolic age, the preaching or proclaiming of the Gospel was part of the

---

[1] There is considerable significance in the use of *offero* absolutely, as in the passage quoted above, and in Tert. de Monog. 10, (a widower) "*offert* annuis diebus dormitionis ejus" (of his deceased wife: cp. Cypr. Ep. 17. 2, "offerre pro illis"). There was no need to explain what was "offered." With the explicit language of Justin and Irenæus before us, it is quite arbitrary to refer the verb simply to prayers or alms, to the exclusion of the Eucharistic elements. Prayers or alms, in fact, were the adjuncts of *the* oblation of the Bread and the Cup. Cp. Clem. Alex. Strom. vi. 113.

ordinary function of Apostles in the first instance, and under them, of evangelists, and of pastors or teachers; yet the exercise of the special *charisma* or gift of prophesying was open, under needful safeguards against disorder, to all who possessed it;[1] and to this fact (neglecting the safeguards) the Montanists appealed in the second half of the second century, under the erroneous assumption that it warranted the extravagant utterances by which they compromised the great name of spiritual freedom.[2] Nor did

---

[1] Duchesne somewhat boldly calls the exercise of this gift of inspired utterance "a liturgy of the Holy Spirit," with its own "real presence and communion." He adds that such "sacred phenomena were extraordinary," and "soon disappeared" (Orig. du Culte, p. 49).

[2] It must not be assumed that all who believed in "visions and revelations" were in principle Montanists. At that rate Cyprian would be so (cp. Church Quarterly Review, xxxii. 78). What differentiated the Montanists on this point from Churchmen was their practical severance of the principle of spirituality from that of order. Tertullian's language as a Montanist, in reference not to doctrine, but to discipline, has a very "*un*conservative tone" (Gore on the Ministry, p. 212).

the scandal thus given deprive the Apostle's precept, as to mutual service through varied gifts,[1] of all significance for the Church in the next age. When Demetrius, bishop of Alexandria, complained that Origen, then one of his laymen, although president of a great catechetical school, had been invited by two bishops of Palestine to address their people, he was told in reply that such a step was not an "innovation," and three precedents were expressly quoted.[2] This is the more remarkable, inasmuch as deacons were very seldom allowed to preach; and even at the end of the fourth century, Jerome had a

---

[1] 1 Pet. iv. 10.
[2] Euseb. vi. 19. But the precedents seem to refer to such preaching in the layman's own diocese. We cannot rely on the "Acts of SS. Lucian and Marcian;" they may have been compiled long after the Decian persecution (Allard, Hist. Perséc. ii. 406); but it is observable that Lucian, being a layman, is made to describe himself as a preacher of Christianity (or "the venerable law") to pagans. Then, " Proconsul dixit: Quo autem officio fungeris ut sis prædicator? Lucianus dixit: Omni animæ consuetudo est lucrari fratrem suum de errore," etc.

sharp word or two for the custom which, "in some churches," forbade the presbyters to preach in their bishop's presence—a custom which obtained in Africa until Valerius of Hippo, relying on Eastern precedents, broke through it in regard to St. Augustine.[1]

(4.)

Another department of Church life in which the mind of the laity could express itself with effect was that of discipline.[2] The primitive layman, as such, contrasted with the modern layman—especially in a "national" Church—in no respect more pointedly than in this, that he was himself subject to discipline, and therefore deeply interested in its exercise. Döllinger's words are worthy of note: "The power of a bishop, and even of a bishop of Rome, was" during the

[1] Cp. Jerome, Ep. 52. 7; Possidius, Vit. S. Aug. 5.
[2] On primitive discipline, cp. below, p. 137.

episcopate of Callistus "the very reverse of absolute: on the contrary, it was limited in its exercise by regard for the feeling and wish of the clergy, especially of the presbytery, and even of the laity."[1] A remarkable instance of this occurs in the story of Novatian. Fabian, bishop of Rome, was minded to ordain him presbyter; but, says his successor Cornelius, "the clergy and many of the laity" strongly objected, on the ground that he was disqualified as having been baptised in illness, and therefore presumably under the fear of death. And the bishop had to "request that he might be allowed" to dispense with the rule in this one instance,[2] on the understanding that it was not to be drawn into a precedent.

An exactly similar exhibition of lay interest in and zeal for discipline took place when Cyprian pressed for the re-admission to

---

[1] Hippolytus und Kallistus, p. 126.
[2] Cornel. in Euseb. vi. 43.

Church-fellowship of persons whose bearing seemed to the laity incompatible with true penitence. He could "hardly persuade" them to consent; and in one or two cases their strong opposition was justified by the results.[1] It is manifest that the laity had it practically in their power to prevent the relaxation of disciplinary rules.

(5.)

Valesius, commenting on the case of Novatian, observes that formerly presbyters could not be ordained by the bishop without

---

[1] Cypr. Ep. 59. 15 (ed. Hartel). The language is very strong. " Vix plebi persuadeo, immo extorqueo. . . . Unus atque alius, obnitente plebe et contradicente, meâ tamen facilitate suscepti," etc. In these cases, we see, lay feeling was not opposed to, but ran strongly in the direction of, strictness. Earlier in this letter Cyprian says, as to the "lax" party, " Viderint laici hoc quomodo curent." It was, indeed, "in præsidentis officio" (Tert. de Pudic. 14) to excommunicate. Yet we hear of Natalius as entreating Zephyrinus, the clergy, and " even the laity," for restoration to communion, and " with difficulty obtaining it" (Anon. in Euseb. v. 28).

the consent of the clergy and people. This principle might be deduced from St. Paul's requirement of "blamelessness" in candidates for the ministry: and Clement of Rome, as we have seen, regards "the consent" or "approval of the whole Church," the entire Christian community in a city, as a condition of regular ordination. And so, a century and a half later, Cyprian reminds his clergy and people that he is accustomed to consult with them as to the qualifications of persons to be ordained;[1] a statement which illustrates the remarks of Tertullian about "probation" of character and "due consideration" as preceding "admission" to ministerial office.[2] And when a bishopric was in question, the laity were not only

---

[1] Cypr. Ep. 38. 1. It is not fair to say that he "only makes this concession to nullify it immediately" (Lightfoot, Dissertations, p. 209). There, and in Ep. 39. 1; 40, he describes certain cases as undeniably exceptional, and therefore calling for a suspension of rule.

[2] Apol. 39; De Præscr. Hær. 43.

called upon to state publicly any objections which they could bring forward against this or that person,—a practice which Alexander Severus admired and applied to the appointment of "provincial governors, or receivers of revenue,"[1]—but the virtual consent of the Church-people of the diocese (or, as it was then called, the "parish,") variously described as "election, request, testimony, judgment or approval,"[2] was a very momentous element in the proceeding. We are not to suppose that man after man voted, in our own modern fashion, for A or for B; but a substantial moral power was exerted in

[1] Lampridius, Vit. Alex. Sev. 45. He uses the now familiar words, "Si quis."

[2] Cp. Peter of Alexandria in Theodoret, H.E. iv. 22, on the three elements of a regular appointment: "a synod of orthodox bishops—the $\psi\tilde{\eta}\phi o\varsigma$ ($=suffragium$) of genuine clergy—the request of the people." This may well represent the ante-Nicene rule. According to the "Hippolytean" canons, the people were to say, "We choose him." For lay *suffragium*, as used by Cyprian, cp. Epp. 55. 8; 59. 5, 6; 67. 4, 5; 68. 2. In Ep. 73. 22, "suffragatores" = supporters.

the earnest, resolute, and often importunate expression of lay opinion or desire, as was afterwards seen in the case of St. Athanasius,[1] although the final responsibility rested neither with the laity nor with the clergy, whose influence was also potent, but with the bishops of the province, as we may infer indeed from the Latin Church rule, " Let no one be *given* as a bishop to an unwilling people."[2] So Cyprian, referring to Numb. xx. 25, says that it was by " Divine direction that a priest should be chosen under the eyes of all, and be approved as worthy and fit by public judgment and testimony, . . . so that, in the presence of the people, either the crimes of the bad might be detected, or the merits of the good be proclaimed, and

---

[1] Apol. c. Arian. 6 : "Give us Athanasius !" Origen, c. Cels. viii. 75, refers to the custom of constraining well-qualified persons to become bishops, when in their excessive modesty they shrunk from such a charge (cp. Euseb. vi. 11).

[2] Celestine I., Ep. 2. 5.

so the ordination might be just and lawful, as having been performed after due inquiry with the suffrage and judgment of all."[1]

(6.)

It remains to consider the relation of the laity to what is called Synodical action. And first, we must not infer too much from such phrases as "meetings of the faithful" —for instance, in Asia Minor—on the Montanist question, when the arguments on behalf of the "new prophesying" were discussed, and its claims deliberately set aside.[2] Naturally, the bishops would consult the well-informed laity on such a point, especially when it was the Montanists' line to disparage

[1] Cypr. Ep. 67. 4. "Judgment" here means deliberate opinion. He adds that the people for whom a bishop is to be chosen "are most fully acquainted by their own observation with the conduct of each individual."

[2] Anon. in Euseb. v. 16. Cp. Tertullian's statement as to Greek councils in which "the whole Christian name is represented," and "questions treated of for the common benefit" (de Jejun. 13).

episcopal authority. But it does not follow that laymen were, in modern phrase, "constituent members" of the assemblies then held, which were evidently identical in constitution with the "compact bodies" of bishops, who, as Eusebius tells us, took part in the Paschal controversy.[1] At any one of these ancient synods, either clerics (as Malchion at Antioch[2]) or laics, whose opinion or advice was deemed specially worth having, might be invited to speak, and what they said would have weight; but the synods properly consisted of bishops

[1] Euseb. v. 23.
[2] So Origen twice in Arabia, and Athanasius at Nicæa. Our first English synod, under Theodore's guidance, followed the ancient precedents. It was a "concilium episcoporum, una cum ... magistris ecclesiæ pluribus" (Bede, iv. 5). But only bishops, and delegates of an absent bishop, passed and signed the resolutions at Herutford. To quote passages about the duty of consulting either clergy or laity as proofs of their co-ordinate synodical right is irrelevant, until it is shown that they could not advise or express opinion without such a right. Manifestly they could do so.

alone.[1] This will perhaps seem too plain a proof of the success of hierarchical usurpation; but the share which, as we have just seen, laymen as well as clerics took in the choice of their bishops would constitute a very close and effective relation between the chief pastor and "all estates of men" in the Church over which he presided. He knew his people, as he knew his presbyters and his deacons; he lived among them, was their ordinary or principal teacher and minister of sacraments, could naturally and habitually identify himself with their mind and their interests, and thus could appropriately act in synod as their spokesman, their advocate, in a real sense

[1] Deputies of absent bishops would sit as bishops. Abp. Potter says, "All the bishops of the province were summoned to provincial councils, and had decisive voices, which, in case of sickness or other lawful impediment, they sometimes gave by proxies; whereas the rest, whether clergy or people, neither had decisive voices, nor were all present, either in person or by their proxies," etc. (Ch. Gov., p. 225).

their representative.¹ If they belonged to him, he belonged not less to them. And this is illustrated by the well-known language of that illustrious prelate of the third century, who is often accused of having developed an episcopal precedency into an episcopal autocracy, and thereby made himself an early instance of the subtle snares of ecclesiastical ambition. But the episcopate, when Cyprian assumed its duties, was more than a mere precedency. Not long before the troubles which forced him into a strenuous assertion of his "ruling" or "directing" authority,² the great Alexandrian who in earlier life had suffered from the arbitrariness of an unfriendly prelate compared the presbytery in each city to its "senate," and the

---

[1] Perhaps the most striking instance of the freedom with which bishops in synod could assume the concurrence of their people is the address of the great Council of Antioch in 269, where the bishops speak for themselves, and also for "presbyters and deacons, *and the churches of God*" (Euseb. vii. 30).

[2] Cypr. Ep. 59. 2.

bishop to its "governor."[1] Nor can it be said that this "high and Divine power," which Cyprian claimed as inherent in the episcopate, was larger than that which St. Paul had entrusted to his own "vicars;" and, in the words of Archbishop Benson, he believed from the very first that he "read the doctrine" of episcopal "inheritance from the Apostles in Scripture as a whole," and "regarded his office as a line traced in the Divine plan, indicated and assumed, if not defined, in the New Testament.[2]" And *therefore* it was happily inevitable that whereas episcopal government, if put in force apart from the Pauline idea of the Church as in union with Christ, would too easily be

---

[1] Orig. c. Cels. iii. 30. In viii. 75 he speaks of those who are called προστάται of the Church as ἄρχοντες. Bishop Pearson (Min. Works, ii. 510) illustrates this use of ἄρχων by Orig. in Jerem. hom. 2, where a bishop is described as entrusted with ecclesiastical rule (ἀρχήν) over all: so that Origen was not thinking of the Athenian "archons for the year."

[2] Abp. Benson, Cyprian, pp. 39, 32.

perverted to the ends of ecclesiastical tyranny—a perversion writ large in the record of worldly-minded prelates—that fatal tendency was barred in the case of the great bishop of Carthage by a habit of mind which made it as natural for him to say, "The bishop is in the Church," as to say, "The Church is in the bishop,"[1] because the relation of both to "the Head" and "the Bishop of souls" was so deeply impressed on his religious consciousness. Let Dr. Pusey's words bring home this point: "Episcopal authority, apart from the doctrine of the mystical unity of the Church, would be liable to be secular, arbitrary, despotic: in connection with it, it . . . is essentially spiritual, parental, self-sacrificing. . . . The bishop, independent in authority, was one organic whole with the Church. It belonged, then, to the oneness of the Church, that whatever was

---

[1] Both sayings come in one sentence of Cypr. Ep. 66. 8.

done should emanate from her oneness and love, as the result of a concordant will, not be accepted only by a cold unparticipating obedience. The maxim, accordingly, of St. Ignatius for the people, to 'do nothing without the bishop,' finds in St. Cyprian the counterpart for the bishop, 'do nothing without the presbytery and the concurrence of the people.'"[1] And so when he says that "from the outset of his episcopate he had made it a rule never to act on his own individual judgment without the counsel of the clergy and the consent of the people,"[2] one may be sure that this resolve expressed for him a moral obligation. In letters to the laity he promises to obtain their "judgment" on individual cases of Christians, who, having "lapsed" in the persecution, now sought

---

[1] Pusey, Pref. to St. Cyprian's Epistles, p. xiv. (Lib. F.).
[2] Cypr. Ep. 14. 4. Of course we cannot infer from these two terms that the clergy had less influence, less of "auctoritas," than the laity.

restoration to Church fellowship.[1] Again, he says that this question will be treated as a whole when the bishops are able to assemble with the clergy, and *also* in presence of "the people as consisting of those who have stood fast, and who are to be held in honour because of their faith and godly fear;"[2] even as afterwards, while magnifying the episcopal office, he ascribes to "the people, as abiding within the Church, a faithful and uncorrupt *majesty;*"[3] and so elsewhere he says that a particular case of three clerics must be fully considered, "not only with his colleagues, but with the entire people itself."[4] The laity would naturally have opportunities of

[1] "Judicantibus," "arbitrium," Ep. 17. 1; 43. 7. Cf. Ep. 67. 4, "judicio" in election of "priests."

[2] Ep. 19. 2. This, as Hefele says, implies that the clergy were in a closer relation to the bishops in synod than were the laity. So Ep. 71. 1: "Coepiscopi cum conpresbyteris qui aderant censuerimus." And more distinctly, Ep. 1: "Conpresbyteri nostri qui nobis adsidebant."

[3] Ep. 59. 18.

[4] Ep. 34. 4.

knowing the specialties of these cases, and their opinion on the application of discipline, in which, as we have seen, they were directly interested, would have a proportionate value. When the proposed council met in the April of 251, we cannot doubt that clerics and laymen alike were present, and that their mind was duly ascertained. Even if Cyprian had wished to gather his colleagues around him within closed doors, it would have been practically impossible for him thus to falsify his own reiterated assurances; but while quoting from a letter of the Roman clergy, which expressed their agreement with his programme, he distinctly attributes the "balanced and moderate resolutions" arrived at to a *copiosus episcoporum numerus*.[1] In other words, the synod was, as usual, composed of bishops, who, in forming their decision, took full account of the opinion alike of clergy and of laity. It is most probable,

---

[1] Ep. 55. 6. Cp. Ep. 73. 1.

indeed, that the decision exactly reflected the opinion thus expressed.

But we must look for a moment at another of the questions which troubled Cyprian's episcopate. I have quoted our late Primate; and the love and honour which enshrine his memory make one very loth to criticise any of his judgments on a chapter of history which, for years, was the resource of his too brief intervals of leisure. But on two or three points it is difficult to follow even Archbishop Benson:[1] and one of them arises

---

[1] For instance, it seems by no means proved that Tertullian's idea of such an "essential priesthood, inherent in all Christians," as qualified laymen to celebrate in default of a presbyter, was the doctrine of the African Church when Cyprian became a presbyter; particularly when one observes that Cyprian, writing as a bishop three years later, goes so far as to allow penitents at the point of death to be, as we should say, absolved by a deacon if a presbyter cannot be found (Ep. 18. 1), but says nothing about a layman. And certainly "the right to approach the Father with prayers and intercessions" could not of itself involve a right to act as the organ of the Christian body corporate. Nor, again, is it clear that Cyprian would have rejected "with disdain and

out of the controversy on heretics' baptism which came before the last three of Cyprian's Carthaginian synods. We all know that the rigorist view, which these councils formulated under his predominant influence, was set aside by the general mind of the West at the great Council of Arles, and was long

horror the title of Pontiff" (Benson, p. 33). Pontifex is simply the Latin equivalent of high-priest; and in Ep. 3, and Ep. 59. 4, it is implied that the Jewish pontifex has a counterpart in the Church, and Cyprian's deacon Pontius (assuming the "Life of Cyprian" to be his) calls him "Christi et Dei pontifex" (c. 9). The title is used of prophets in the "Teaching," c. 13; and Hippolytus (?) claims to inherit the Apostles' "high-priesthood" (Refut. Hæres. Prœm.) Nor is it the case that with Cyprian, Christian presbyters answer to Levites, and bishops alone to priests (p. 35). In Ep. 63. 14, the words "utique ille sacerdos vice Christi fungitur . . . et sacrificium verum . . . tunc offert" cannot be restricted to bishops; for in Ep. 5 it is assumed that presbyters will "offer" when visiting confessors in prison. Further, Ep. 1 clearly implies that presbyters, such as Faustinus, are "sacerdotes;" Ep. 40 uses "sacerdotibus" in reference to newly ordained presbyters; Ep. 61. 3 speaks of presbyters as "cum episcopo sacerdotali honore conjuncti;" Ep. 67. 4 says, "Nec hoc in episcoporum tantum *et* sacerdotum, sed *et* in diaconorum ordinationibus."

afterwards treated by St. Augustine as erroneous. Are we to say that the mistake thus corrected was due to the non-consultation of the laity, and that Cyprian took a wrong line because, on these occasions, he did not "redeem his early pledge"?[1] What, then, was that pledge? To "*do* nothing," evidently in the way of diocesan administration,[2] "without taking the advice of the clergy and obtaining the assent of the laity." The question of the lapsed was such a point: it was, indeed, very much a layman's question. Shall the faithful hereafter stand wholly aloof from the lapsed, however penitent; or shall the lapsed, after so much penance has been fulfilled, be restored to communion with the faithful?[3] But the second question was (1) wider than the area of diocesan work,

---

[1] Benson, p. 431.

[2] The verb used is *gerere*.

[3] Indiscriminate "admission to communion ... is very often a scandal to communicants, and was wont, among ourselves, to be one of the taunts of dissenters" (Pusey, The Councils of the Church, etc., p. 76).

and (2) distinctly doctrinal or theological.[1] It affected the administration of the great initiatory sacrament, and, underlying it, the far-reaching issue—Does heresy invalidate sacramental ministration? Are the official acts of an ordained man void, when done outside the unity of the faith and of the Church? It could hardly be maintained that all the laity as such were competent to pronounce on such a matter along with the bishops; and if only some laics were thus competent, we have a laity within a laity, and the broad ground of equal right in synod for bishops, clergy, and lay communicants, is abandoned. As a matter of fact, when Cyprian presided over his seventh and last Council on September 1, 256, the record distinctly says that the eighty-seven bishops had with them presbyters and deacons, and

---

[1] Abp. Benson says that the two questions were "analogous as questions of dogmatic discipline" (p. 431). Surely this confuses a clear distinction.

that "a very large part of the people were also present,"[1]—so that even here the principle of inviting the presence of laity as well as of clergy was fully maintained, although the bishops, as before, were the "constituents" of the synod; and if the laity are supposed to be wronged by not having been admitted to actual membership,[2] the position of the

---

[1] "A vast laity" (Benson, p. 365). Further on, p. 426, "We cannot but deem that it was among them principally" that the view which in the next century corrected Cyprian's stern doctrine was forming itself. Is there any evidence for this? We know that the Africans "followed their own law" up to A.D. 314, when a "plenary" Western Council decided against it (cp. the first Council of Arles, can. 8; Augustine, de Bapt. ii. 14). On this point, see a good note in Mr. Rackham's Essay (Ch. Reform, p. 53).

[2] Some points in Mr. Rackham's comment on Cyprianic letters in regard to lay *status* may here be noticed together, in the order in which they occur in his essay. He says that Cyprian "read the letter announcing Cornelius' election" as bishop of Rome to "'all the brethren' *then sitting in council*," and refers us to Ep. 45. 2, 3. But what Cyprian says is, that the election was made "known to the brethren," *i.e.* his episcopal colleagues, "*and* to the whole people here." And the context does not exhibit the representatives of the laity as "sitting in

clergy in that respect differed only in degree from their own.

council." It is "God's priests" (*i.e.* bishops) who are described as "sitting together;" the laity are present as spectators and auditors, as Abp. Benson's account of this first council of Carthage implies (p. 130), and, as Mr. Rackham says afterwards, "as a reverent crowd." Again, as to a Roman synod held by Cornelius to receive back some confessors who had repented of schism, Cornelius is quoted as saying that, when he and his presbyters had accepted that submission, it "followed of necessity" that this acceptance should be made known to the Roman laity, and "accordingly 'a great concourse of the people met together,' and the confessors were publicly received back into the Church." Here something is put in, and more is left out. Cornelius does not say "of necessity," but merely "Quod erat consequens" (Ep. 49. 2). And as to the public gathering—it clearly took place in order that the people at large might be present at, and testify their approval of, the solemn act of rehabilitation by their prelate and his presbyters. The act of submission was read, and then Cornelius "commanded" one of the confessors to resume his forfeited "place; cæteris, cum ingenti populi *suffragio* [*i.e.* approval], omnia ante gesta remisimus Deo," etc. The case of two "libellatic" Spanish bishops (Ep. 67) is confessedly "extreme," and analogous to that of a bishop who fell into open heresy, in which case it was held that the Catholic laity ought to forsake his ministrations. Cyprian's language (Ep. 69. 14) on grace, as "poured forth on all without respect of persons," is quite irrelevant to the matter in

(7.)

Such, on the whole, was the position of the primitive laity.[1] It doubtless contrasts

hand; it has nothing to do with lay rights or powers in regard to Church administration; it refers to the case of the so-called "clinics," who had been baptised (as was Novatian) on a sick-bed, by simple affusion. When we are told that Cyprian addresses his people "not as his flock, but as his 'brothers,'" it is natural to ask, Where is the antithesis? And did not his people know, as of course, that they *were* the "flock" and he was the "pastor"? (cp. Ep. 66. 8). To take only one other point: "We have the normal composition of a council—'bishops, presbyters, deacons, confessors, together with the faithful laity'—recognised as such by the Roman clergy, and serving as the type of a council to be held at Rome." The letter (Ep. 30. 5) speaks, not of a council in the "normal" sense, but of a conference (*conlatione consiliorum*) held between the several classes named, on the subject of the lapsed, whose cases, of course, would be very diverse. In such conferences the laity would naturally take a specially active part, and their concurrence would be expressly required and given.

[1] Mr. Keble wrote to a correspondent, "The voice of the laity, in one form or another, has always been a most essential part of the voice of the whole Church. Even in the most vital case of fundamental doctrine, the Church diffusive, in which the laity are included, has a kind of veto, as I understand it, on the decision of a General Council. . . . Now, if they (the laity) have a

very startlingly with that of the *plebs sancta* — to borrow a phrase from the canon of the Mass[1]—in the modern Church of Rome. There the non-cleric is, apparently, supposed to have no concern in ecclesiastical questions; and his ecclesiastical obligations consist in obedience to certain "precepts." But if we compare the ancient lay *status* with the Anglican, as it exists under the conditions of "establishment," we encounter anomalies of a different kind.

---

negative voice, it is not, *primâ facie*, essential at what stage in the discussion that voice is permitted to be heard" (Letters of Spirit. Counsel, p. 296). He refers to an article contributed by him to the Christian Remembrancer of October 1851, in which, while holding that the laity of the ancient Church were not members of synods, he says that "they seem to have exercised without limit the indirect power of demanding that the cause" (in questions of doctrine) "be reheard in another synod, etc."

[1] It occurs in the oblation, after the words of institution: "Wherefore, O Lord, we Thy servants, and also (*sed et*) Thy holy people, being mindful," etc., "do offer to Thy glorious majesty, out of (*de*) Thine own gifts . . . a pure sacrifice," etc. The liturgy of St. Basil quotes 1 Pet. ii. 9 shortly before the words of institution.

The primitive layman, as such, was supposed to be a weekly communicant : he was one of "a flock adhering to its own shepherd," as St. Cyprian words it ;[1] he knew exactly where he stood as a Christian and a Churchman; his position kept him constantly in touch with all the spiritual questions and tasks which concerned the body to which he belonged, and the officials who repaid his support by frankest confidence. If he fell into grave sin, he knew that he was amenable to a discipline which would severely test his repentance. At any moment he might be called upon to give the most effective of all possible guarantees as to his religious loyalty and constancy; and if he failed in this stern trial, he forfeited the privileges of Church-fellowship. But how is it now in England? We have, indeed, very many laymen to whom the idea of "a royal priesthood" is very different from a mere

---

[1] Ep. 66. 8.

exclusion of "sacerdotalism" in the clergy; who, with a splendid whole-heartedness, use to the full their peculiar opportunities of serving the Lord in their several vocations, in their varying spheres of Church life, without the suspicion of a "professional" aim. Such men, whatever may be, in the current phrase, their "school of thought," are laymen in very deed, laymen in spirit and truth, laymen worthy of the title, whose advice on many Church subjects, whose co-operation in wide areas of Church business, would be just as valuable under modern conditions as those of the *stantes* could be to Cyprian. But the difficulty consists in this, that any man may call himself, if he pleases, "a lay member of the national Church," not only without assimilating its historical principles, but even without accepting its creed or participating in its ordinances.[1]

[1] "Every English layman may claim membership in the Church of England, irrespective of dogmatic belief"

Discipline does not exist for him;[1] he need not even, *de facto*, be a communicant; he *may* be, as it has been caustically expressed, contentedly "in a fog" on great questions of Church order, or ready to pronounce offhand on theological points which he has never really studied; while such a state of mind is obviously the reverse of a qualification for administering ecclesiastical "government." And the problem which confronts us,—even without estimating the vast reach of the civil power in regard to Church doctrine or ritual,—is how to guard the

(Bodley's France, i. 139). The writer means "every English citizen." The confusion of ideas, under which "parishioners" and "laymen" can be treated as convertible terms, has grown up since Church and nation ceased to be co-extensive, *i.e.* since Hooker's view ceased to have any practical interest.

[1] On popular aversion to the idea of "discipline," cp. Strong's Bamp. Lect. p. 352 ff. "The right of the Church to exercise discipline seems to break into the charmed circle of individual independence," etc. Yet the "Ordering of Priests" supposes that "the discipline of Christ" will in some form exist, to be "ministered" along with "doctrines and sacraments."

moral rights of those laymen who fulfil responsibilities from being overborne by the number of those who are content to claim privileges. Let us hope that our ecclesiastical rulers will be enabled to deal both wisely and loyally with complications which our time has not created but inherited, and which will need full measure of the spirit of right judgment.

ADDRESS III.

(1.)

It has been said that "Christianity came into the world as an idea rather than an institution," and had to take time to fit itself out with the appliances which could verify the prophetic description of it as a kingdom, or its own pretension to be a society. Antitheses usually require some cross-examination; and if, as we have seen, Christ did establish the Apostleship, He thereby provided His Church, from its very birth, with an institution most momentous in character. Institutions could not be inappropriate, could not but be congenial, to a faith which resolves itself into the confession of the Word made flesh, of Deity enshrined in a human frame. Such a faith would be but consistent in hallowing outward things to be media of inward benefit. And if the restriction of the word "Sacrament," in our popular theological language, to the two great rites which Christ expressly instituted, has tended somewhat to the disparagement of other ordinances in which the outward sign and the inward grace are combined, as confirmation or ordination, it has at any rate served as a helpful reminder of the close relation of Baptism and the Eucharist to the personal action and will of Our Lord.[1] Baptism is represented in Matt. xxviii. 19 as initiating the recipient into the deepest sanctities of the new faith,—as uniting him to the Father, the Son, and the Holy Spirit, thus revealed. In the Acts it is regarded as a means of "washing away sin:" in the Epistles, of putting away sin by the virtue of Christ's

[1] Tertullian states the general sacramental principle in De Res. Carn. 8: "Cum anima Deo allegitur, ipsa (caro) est quæ efficit ut anima allegi possit: scilicet caro abluitur, ut anima emaculetur," etc.

"death," and of "putting on Christ," that is, appropriating His presence in the renewal of spiritual energy; and it is clearly alluded to as a "bath of regeneration,"—a phrase which echoes the great saying of Our Lord on the necessity of being "born again of water and Spirit." So the primitive Christians speak: Justin Martyr uses "regenerated" as a synonym for "baptised," describes the rite as performed in his day, and adds that it is also called "illumination"—a title suggested by, or alluded to in, two passages of the Epistle to the Hebrews.[1] Another term for it was the "seal," as when a metrical epitaph (of Abercius) in the second century describes the Christians of Rome as "a people having a bright seal;" and in the same sense, Eusebius speaks of "the seal in the Lord."[2] This high idea of baptism

---

[1] Heb. vi. 4; x. 32. So Clement of Alexandria (Quis Dives, 42, ap. Euseb. iii. 23) uses ἐφώτισε for the administration of baptism; and cp. his Pæd. i. 26.

[2] Euseb. vi. 5. The seal is here no mere pledge of

Its Administration.

carried with it the necessity of careful preliminary instruction and probation:[1] and hence the "catechetical" system was developed; hence, also, before the actual immersion[2] in water, the candidate, in reply to solemn interrogations, renounced the devil, professed the faith, and promised obedience.[3] But other authorities imply that infants are susceptible of baptism: one great but erratic

Divine favour, or ratification of a covenant, but an expression of Divine ownership: cp. Pusey on Holy Baptism, p. 137. Clement of Alexandria, in Quis Dives, 42, applies the term to baptism, but in Strom. ii. 11, to what we call confirmation: so Cyprian, Ep. 73. 9, and Cornelius ap. Euseb. vi. 43.

[1] Tertullian blames the hasty and superficial training of catechumens among the "heretics" (De Præscr. Hær. 41). Origen says that, while philosophers address any one indiscriminately, Christians test beforehand the souls of those who wish to hear them, and form two classes—one for beginners, the other for those who have given proof of their intention to wish for nothing but what Christians approve (c. Cels. iii. 51).

[2] This was the regular method; but in case of sickness affusion was allowed (cp. above, p. 94).

[3] On these interrogations and answers, cp. Tert. de Cor. 3, de Bapt. 6; Hippol. Canons, 122 ff.; cp. Cypr. Ep. 69. 7.

writer, who disliked the practice, is himself a witness to its frequency;[1] it is ascribed by Origen to apostolic tradition,[2] and explained by Cyprian as supposing a transmission of the taint of sinfulness antecedently to actual transgression, so that even for babes baptism retains its character as given for "remission of sins."[3] And baptism into the name of the Trinity—baptism as the start of a new spiritual life—could not but bring the recipient into union with the Holy Spirit; but it was followed, as soon as possible, by that laying on of "apostolic" hands which had been ranked among the "first principles" of Christianity, and was believed to convey that fuller influence of the Spirit of ghostly strength, which makes its name

---

[1] Tertull. de Bapt. 18. He advised postponement of baptism, not only in the case of "parvuli," but also in the case of all unmarried persons; the ground of this peculiar counsel being the "weighty" importance of baptism as the conveyance of a "divina substantia."

[2] Hom. 14 in Luc.; in Rom. lib. 5. c. 9.

[3] Ep. 64. 5.

of Confirmation, if rightly understood, so true.[1] References in Scripture to the Spirit's action under the figure of "anointing" would naturally suggest to the next century the use of chrism in this rite. It could not then be foreseen that the supplementary ceremony would ultimately go far to efface the original outward sign.[2]

The great Sacrament which St. Paul describes as a means of "communion with," or "participation of," the Body and Blood of Christ—that body which he speaks of as to be "discriminated" from common food, and as insulted by the sacrilege of unworthy

---

[1] On "the relation of Confirmation to Baptism," cp. Church Quarterly Review, xlv. p. 357 ff.

[2] Tertullian is the first to speak of unction as applied in confirmation (before the imposition of hands). He represents it, not as prescribed by Apostles, but as suggested by the anointings in the Old Testament. The Greek Church absolutely calls confirmation "the mystery of the holy chrism;" and the application of chrism is the only imposition of hands in her rite. The Latin "Catechismus ad Parochos," when affirming chrism to be "the matter of this sacrament," claims "very many fathers," but names only the pseudo-Dionysius and one of the False Decretals (ii. 3. 7).

reception—came ere long to be called "Eucharist," although at first that name would indicate the service of highest thanksgiving which grew up around it, and through which the worshippers passed to the highest privilege of their Christianity. In the apostolic age it was celebrated, as it had been instituted, in the evening, which, according to the Jewish reckoning, was the beginning of a new day—that day being ordinarily the first in the week; and at Corinth it was preceded by a supper, intended to recall and imitate that solemn meal in the upper chamber during which, in regard to the Bread, and after which, in regard to the Cup, the "new Passover" had been ordained. This supper, "resembling the Lord's,"[1] was also commemorative of

[1] St. Augustine repeatedly uses the phrase of 1 Cor. i. 20 as referring to the Eucharist itself (Ep. 54. 7 : De Serm. Dom. in Monte, ii. 2. 26; in Joan. Ev. Tr. 50. 10). Yet there is reason to think that this is exegetically an error. The words of St. Paul are, "When you assemble together, it is not (possible) to eat *a* 'supper of the

His new commandment, and thus acquired the name of "love-feast" or "Agape;" but about the close of the first century it appears to have been, at least in some places, detached from the Eucharist, which became the characteristic feature of a meeting for worship in the early morning, when the Roman day, as distinct from the Jewish, had begun.[1] Ignatius requires the bishop's

Lord,' *for* each of you while eating is taking his own supper before others," etc. He means—You profess to imitate the Lord's meal in the upper chamber, but your disorderly behaviour nullifies the profession; a series of selfishly snatched meals, often characterised by "drunkenness," is not a "supper like His." But the Eucharist, however it might be profaned, would not lose its character: that very character would bring down "judgment" on such misuse. Moreover, the "supper" clearly consisted of other food beside bread and wine (cp. Dict. Chr. Antiq. I. 40). Cp. The Scriptural and Primitive Time for the Celebration, by Presbyter Anglicanus, p. 10 ff.

[1] The natural sense of Pliny's report to Trajan on this point is, that witnesses who said they had ceased for years (some even for twenty years) to be Christians, in telling what they knew of Christian observances, affirmed that at the time as to which they could testify, there was a purely religious meeting at dawn on a stated day, and at a later hour a common meal; but that the latter had been

sanction alike for Eucharist and for Agape.[1] Of the former, he says that heretics are quite abandoned when Pliny (by Trajan's order) had prohibited *hetæriæ* or clubs (on which cp. Origen, c. Cels. i. 1). The early morning assembly can hardly have been other than Eucharistic, as Tertullian many years later observes (de Cor. 3) that although the Eucharist was instituted at supper-time, it is now received at meetings held "*even* before daybreak." So that here in Pliny's account we have (1) the "early celebration" on Sundays, (2) the supper or Agape on Sunday evenings. The two had been thus distinctively observed before the prohibition, which was itself prior to the persecution of A.D. 112. The prohibition had been obeyed by a suspension of the Agape, which had no such indispensable character as the Eucharist. But it would naturally be resumed when danger was over. So the writer of the epistle to Diognetus says, "We have a common table" (c. 5.), and Tertullian, as a Catholic, praises the Church Agapæ; but when Montanism has jaundiced his mind, he vituperates them in his coarse fashion—" It is in saucepans that your 'love' glows" (De Jejun. 17): a taunt which, one must own, some words of Clem. Alex. tend to justify (Pæd. ii. 4). Abuses, like those at Corinth, did creep in at these meals, even when they were associated with commemoration of saints; and hence it was that the Council of Laodicea prohibited them, and St. Ambrose, at Milan, had to let Monica know that he had forbidden all eating and drinking at martyr-shrines (Aug. Confess. vi. 2; cp. Ep. 22. 3; 29. 2 ff.). Anniversary Agapæ were often held in catacombs (see Lanciani, Pag. and Chr. Rome, p. 336).

[1] Lightfoot insists that in the words, "It is not

consistent in "not acknowledging it to be the flesh of our Saviour which suffered for our sins," inasmuch as they do not allow that He had real flesh : he puts the two negations into parallelism.[1] Justin Martyr, several

permissible either to baptise or to hold an Agape apart from the bishop" (Smyrn. 8), "the Agape must include the Eucharist." Why so, when the necessity of the bishop's agency or sanction for a "valid" or legitimate Eucharist had been insisted on in the sentence but one before? Cp. above, p. 65.

[1] Smyrn. 6. Holding this belief as to the Eucharist, Ignatius could afford to call the gospel, or faith, "Christ's flesh," or love, His "blood" (Philad. 5. Trall. 8; Rom. 7) with the thought that in the gospel He was evidently set forth, or that faith and love were directed towards, or sustained by, His humanity. To gloss Trall. 8., as Lightfoot does, by saying that faith and love are "the substance" and "the energy of the Christian life" (though he admits an "indirect reference to the Eucharist"), is virtually to substitute "the Church's flesh" for "the Lord's." We see at once what Ignatius means when he says that the "knowledge of God is Jesus Christ" (Eph. 17, etc.): condensed sayings of this sort are "his way," and, with his habit of looking the Incarnation habitually in the face, it would be natural to him to use Eucharistic terms, in a derivative sense, for those dispositions on which depends all vital communion with the Incarnate, and especially that which has the Eucharist for its channel and sphere. Lightfoot will not even allow

years later, describes the Sunday Eucharist at some length, expressly mentioning the "president"[1] as the officiant, dwelling on the prolonged act of thanksgiving which preceded the actual administration, and informing us that water was mingled with the wine.[2] He has already asserted, as matter of Christian "teaching," a certain parallelism between the Incarnation and the Eucharist; "Jesus, through the Word," assumes "flesh and blood for our salvation," and the sacred food which we receive, and "by assimilating

"the bread of God," in Eph. 5, to have a "direct" reference to the Eucharist. He does admit a special Eucharistic reference in the words of Eph. 20, "breaking one bread, which is a medicine of immortality"; yet even here, as if to guard against "sacramentalism," the Agape must needs be brought in. How could any other food than the Bread and Cup of the Lord be a means of "preservation of body and soul to everlasting life"?

[1] Τῷ προεστῶτι τῶ ἀδελφῶν (Apol. i. 65), meaning the bishop (or in his absence the presbyter).

[2] So in the epitaph of Abercius, "Faith giving a mixed drink with bread." Clement of Alexandria alludes to the mixture in Pædag. i. 47. Cp. also Iren. v. 2. 3.

which our flesh is nourished,[1] is the flesh and blood of that Jesus who became flesh"—in that, as Dorner explains the thought of the passage, He renders it the "organ of His activity and self-communication"; and Justin ascribes this effect to "a prayer of" or dependent on "a word which is from Him," a thanksgiving leading up to the words of institution.[2] As Clement had referred to the "offering of the gifts," so Justin speaks of the elements as "offered up" to God;[3]

---

[1] This seems to be the scene of κατὰ μεταβολὴν in Justin, Apol. i. 66.

[2] The Lord's prayer is not a "thanksgiving."

[3] Dial. 41. 70. Ποιεῖν there must needs mean to "offer," as in LXX., Exod. xxix. 36, or Lev. iv. 20 (of things offered). Justin undoubtedly regards the Eucharistic offering as made by the whole Church, through the agency of the "president" who officiates. Ignatius does not say that the Eucharist is a sacrifice; but he frequently speaks of "altar," or place of sacrifice, as when he says that "if a man is not within the altar" (-place) "he lacketh the bread of God" (Eph. 5); or explains the being "outside the altar" by "doing anything apart from bishop and presbytery and deacons" (Trall. 7). Lightfoot takes these phrases "metaphori-

and Irenæus, who in effect repeats his doctrinal account with more fulness and more distinctness, calls this service "the new oblation of the New Covenant, which the Church receiving from the Apostles

cally" of "the Church," "the congregation lawfully gathered together under its appointed officers." But why call the Church an altar-place, unless its worship were in a true sense sacrificial? And if that worship culminated in the Eucharist, why generalise the sacrifice here implied into mere "prayer," instead of giving to "prayer" its full intensity of significance? In Magnes. 7, "come together all of you as to one temple" (of God), "as to one altar, to one Jesus Christ," there is no need for taking Christ Himself to be the altar in view. No doubt a metaphorical sense, analogous to that of St. Paul's words in Phil. ii. 17, is indicated in Ign. Rom. 2. But the governing passage as to this term is Philad. 4, "Be careful then to observe" (only) "one Eucharist, for there is one flesh of our Lord Jesus Christ, and one cup unto union with His blood—one altar, as" (there is) "one bishop." Even here, reference to "altar" is glossed as "probably" meaning an assembly for worship. If this "spiritualising" method were applied to a class of passages relating, say, to the Incarnation, what would be the result? Lightfoot says that in the second century the lay communicants did not stand "within the altar-place." But we know that even in the third they *did* "stand by the table" itself (cp. Dionysius of Alexandria ap. Euseb. vii. 9). Observe that Tertullian can say, "Nos enim sumus et templa Dei

offers to God throughout the world."[1] The form of liturgy used was very elastic: scope

et altaria" (de Cor. 9); but no one can doubt that when he speaks of the "ara Dei" and the "sacrificium" in De Orat. 19, he means the Lord's table and the Eucharist in its "oblatory" aspect.

[1] Iren. iv. 17. 5; cp. Iren. Fr. 38. The outward elements were the immediate matter of the oblation, but after "receiving the invocation" (iv. 18. 5), the bread was "no longer common bread, but Eucharist, consisting of two things—an earthly and an heavenly." And the like, it is implied, took place as to the cup, so that the elements, remaining bread and wine, became associated with the body and blood of the Lord. Irenæus' point against the Gnostics is, "*You* cannot offer the Eucharist to the Father, because (1) the elements, in your view, are not of His creating; (2) you deny a future resurrection, whereas the Eucharist implies that the communicants' bodies are endued with a principle of eternal life." He says that "the altar is in heaven," meaning that the oblation is thither directed (compare the "Supplices te rogamus" in the Roman mass); but on his own showing the table on which the bread and cup were placed must be subordinately an altar. Of course, in this idea of Eucharistic sacrifice there was not even an approach to the notion of a reiteration of the one atoning sacrifice of Christ. And Irenæus, like Justin, asserts the priestly character of the Christian body as a whole (iv. 8. 3; v. 34. 3): the offering, he says, is made by "the Church;" but it was perfectly consistent with this that the holy words involving or

was allowed for extempore prayer,[1] and there would be considerable variety in tone and expression, together with a general identity of order. The service was divided into two parts. The first, at which persons preparing for baptism might be present, consisted of readings from Scripture, recitations, singing of psalms, and a sermon.[2] Then those who were not in communion with the Church went out: the solemn prayers of the faithful began, the elements were brought to the celebrant, and he made over them the long and detailed thanksgiving already referred to, concluding, as Irenæus has shown us, with an invocation of the

---

expressing it should be uttered by the bishop or presbyter, officiating as her organ. Cyprian himself says, referring to all Churchmen, "We come together with the brethren, et sacrificia divina cum Dei sacerdote celebramus" (de Dom. Orat. 4).

[1] This seems implied by Justin, Apol. i. 67 : cp. Lightfoot, St. Clement, i. 386; Warren, Lit. of Antenicene Church, p. 106.

[2] Cp. Justin, l.c.; Tert. de Anima, 9.

Holy Spirit to sanctify the bread and cup for purposes of communion. Intercession for the departed, as well as for the living, was never omitted; and such brief responsive utterances as began with "Lift up your hearts" may date from the second century.[1] The Pauline Epistles contain some rhythmical sentences which have the ring of primitive hymns; the concluding part of Clement of Rome's Epistle breaks forth into prayers evidently then in use; the doxology in its present form occurs in some old "canons" of Roman Church use already referred to, which also include several prayers,[2] as does the much earlier (so-called) "Teaching of the Apostles"—a Jewish manual

[1] Cyprian mentions the "Sursum Corda" and "Habemus ad Dominum" (Dom. Orat. 31); but an earlier authority gives also the subsequent versicle and response, "Let us give thanks," etc. (Hippolytean Canons, 25-50).

[2] We read of non-eucharistic services (*e.g.* Hipp. Can. 21, 26); but the full "daily office" grew up later (Duchesne, Origines du Culte, p. 433).

Christianised, which also assumes the Eucharist to be a sacrificial service in which *episkopoi* and deacons are to minister; but, as a whole, it implies a very unapostolic conception of the doctrinal purport of Christianity. The remains of the elements were carried by deacons to those who had been unable to attend; but communicants were often allowed to take home with them a portion of the holy bread, and partake of it before the first food of each day.[1]

(2.)

Other observances, such as that of the first day of the week, in memory of the

---

[1] This seems to be the sense of "ante omnem cibum" in Tertull. ad Uxor. ii. 5; cp. de Orat. 13. This "keeping of the Lord's body" at home is mentioned (ib. 19; and Cyprian, de Lapsis, 26. This would tend to make daily celebration exceptional; but in times of special trial it seems to have been usual (cp. Cypr. Ep. 57. 3, a synodal letter, "sacerdotes qui sacrificia Dei quotidie celebramus;" and Tert. de Idol. 7).

Lord's Resurrection, and, in the next century, of the anniversary of that Resurrection as preceded by His atoning death, grew out of the intense interest which, from the very first, was directed towards events on which Christianity depended, and but for which it could not have drawn breath. We have no reason to think that the Lord's Day, or Sunday, as we call it, was literally substituted for Saturday as a new Sabbath; on the contrary, the Sabbath is classed by St. Paul with the new moon observance as belonging to the typical system of Judaism;[1] and the apostolic Council of Jerusalem, while directing Gentile converts in Syria and Cilicia, out of regard for their Jewish fellow-Christians, to abstain from tasting "things strangled" or "blood," significantly refrains from imposing on them a sabbatical observance. In conformity to these texts, Ignatius and Tertullian treat sabbaths as obsolete for

[1] Col. ii. 16.

Christians;[1] and in fact, Saturday, still called the Sabbath, became a minor weekly festival in memory of its old sabbatical character, which therefore was *not* supposed to have been transferred to Sunday. Later, in the West, it gradually became associated with ideas of penitence,[2] such as had early suggested fasting up to 3 p.m. on Wednesdays and Fridays, called "Station-days," apparently by adaptation of a term used for military duty.[3] That the children of the bride-chamber should fast when they

[1] Ignat. Magn. 9; Tertull. de Idol. 14.

[2] "When I go to Rome," said St. Ambrose, "I fast on Sabbath. When I am here"—at Milan—"I do not fast" (Aug. Ep. 54. 3). Cp. Hooker, v. 72. 8. Augustine severely criticised a Roman tract which insisted that Saturday *must* be a fast-day (Ep. 36). This Roman usage seems to have been a transference from Wednesday. Easter-even was everywhere a fast.

[3] Hermas deprecates the observance of "stations" (Sim. v. 1). Clement of Alexandria mentions the fasts on Wednesdays and Fridays (Strom. vii. 75). Tertullian calls them half-fasts (de Jejun. 13). There was always a communion on these days (de Orat. 19).

had lost the Bridegroom's sensible presence, was deemed a matter of course; and a fasting-period of very variable duration became a fitting and helpful prelude to the triumphant joy of the Easter festival,[1] which was to be prolonged through fifty days.[2] Unfortunately that festival was kept with a certain diversity of usage as to the time or day of its celebration, or, as it was expressed, of the "closing of the fast" which preceded it. The majority of Churches[3] took Sunday as the determining point; they would not begin their Easter until the Saturday evening which followed the day of the Jewish Passover, and then they spent the whole night in devotion.[4] The minority

---

[1] Some fasted only one day, others two, others longer; and some, while professing to fast only one day, made it a "day" of forty hours (Irenæus ap. Euseb. v. 24; cp. Tertull. de Orat. 18, and Dion. Alex. Ep. Can.).

[2] Cp. Tertull. de Jejun. 14; de Cor. 3.

[3] Including that of Palestine.

[4] On the great paschal vigil, cp. Tertull. ad Uxor. ii. 4; Euseb. vi. 9.

—the Churches of Proconsular Asia—relying on traditions which they traced to St. John, associated the beginning of their Easter with the Passover evening itself, on whatever day of the week it might fall.[1] They would not conform to the more prevalent usage; they deemed themselves trustees of a custom derived from the beloved disciple; and when Polycarp, who had sat at St. John's feet, and was believed to have been made bishop by his hands,[2] visited Rome in order to confer with its bishop, the two prelates found it best "to agree

---

[1] The suggestion that this tells against the authenticity of the Fourth Gospel—which seems to date the Lord's death on the afternoon of Nisan 14, so that the Lord's Supper would not be assigned to the paschal evening—assumes that the Quartodecimans meant to commemorate that Supper; whereas what they had in mind was the Lord's death, considered as followed by His resurrection. Cp. Bp. Lightfoot on "Supernatural Religion," pp. 17, 245. Moreover, Polycrates of Ephesus quotes John xiii. 25 (Euseb. v. 24).

[2] Tertull. de Præscr. Hær. 32; Irenæus, iii. 3. 4, says "by Apostles."

to differ," and, in token of their undisturbed fraternal concord, Anicetus asked Polycarp to celebrate the Eucharist in his church. It was otherwise with a successor of Anicetus at the end of that second century; he had probably found that the "Asiatic" peculiarity was being introduced into Rome itself,[1] and under this provocation he withdrew his Church from communion with those who, as insisting on the "fourteenth day" of the month Nisan, acquired the name of Quartodecimans; and he furthermore wrote circulars to other bishops, requesting them to follow his example. It is one of the well-known

---

[1] Cp. Salmon, Infallibility of the Church, p. 283. Victor does not appear, in Eusebius' account, as assuming anything like a "papal" attitude; he suspends communion on the part of his own church with the Quartodecimans, and endeavours to induce other churches to do the like. The first (the consent of his clergy and people being assumed) was within his competence: in the latter he failed. But there is no evidence that he attempted to give the law to the churches in general. Cp. the writer's The Roman See in the Early Church, etc., p. 28.

proofs of the non-existence, in those early times, of anything like a supreme jurisdiction attaching to Rome or her bishop, that the leading prelate of the day, with others, remonstrated " somewhat sharply " with Victor, who had consequently to acquiesce in the failure of an ill-advised suggestion.[1]

(3.)

As these observances grew up in close relation to the two great sacraments, so did Baptism and the Eucharist stand forth as images and as outworks of the central faith

---

[1] The purport of Irenæus' celebrated passage on the Roman church was thus expressed, sixty-one years ago, by Archdeacon R. W. Evans: "As she could not but have communication with every church from every quarter, who through their members poured their information into her cistern, she became, independently of her own tradition, the general depository of the tradition of the Catholic Church" (Biogr. of Early Church, i. 256). He applied "potior principalitas" to the Roman *church* as having a "primacy of rank," or an honorary pre-eminence, higher than that of the Alexandrian or Antiochene.

in a really Divine Redeemer. A celebrated writer[1] has described what he calls "the Supper"—a name, one must add, distinctly inadequate—as supplying in "its uninterrupted celebration the first proof of the steadfast faith of the Church in the Divine nature of Christ," and has specified baptism as "the second," in that, being administered "for remission of sins, the basis of which was laid in Christ's propitiatory work, it stood connected with the higher estimate of His Person" as an Atoner because both human and Divine.

It was pre-eminently by these pre-eminent rites that the Church realised its union with Him, and the inestimable "preciousness" of a faith that rested upon Him. For He Himself was, in a deep sense, His religion;[2] it was centred on Him personally, as it could

---

[1] Dorner on the Person of Christ, i. 1. 3. Cp. Pliny—"carmen Christo quasi deo dicere."

[2] Cp. Liddon, Bamp. Lect., pp. 129, 337.

not have been centred on any merely human founder. Christianity, it has been excellently said, appears in the New Testament mainly as "a life;" but the antithesis often set up between a life and a creed is transparently unreal, for "a life must have a background consisting of those beliefs or convictions which determine conduct; and the richer and deeper the life, the richer and deeper the background."[1] Now, the background of Christian life, being a belief about Christ, was essentially doctrinal; that is, it could not but involve an answer to the question, Who and what is Christ, and on what are His claims grounded? Nothing can better illustrate this than the motives employed by St. Paul as a moral teacher. And although he does not put his Christology into a series of propositions, one sees that his Christ is one who can be prayed to, praised, glorified, worshipped. More impressive than those

[1] I avail myself here of a sermon by Prof. Sanday.

sayings of his about his Master's dignity which are quoted as "proof-texts" is the pervading dominant tone of mind which makes him regard Christ as no created being ought to be regarded by men who know what they should mean by the name "God."[1] His relation to his Lord is that of an absolute dependence, an unlimited devotion, a loyalty undistinguishable from that which is due to the Supreme, and which, therefore, could not without virtual idolatry be offered to a fellow-creature, however excellent. Thus

[1] Cp. Dale on the Atonement, p. 24. If the Christianity taught by the original apostles had been Ebionitic, such a fact must have come out in the contest carried on by the Judaising Christians, who professed to adhere to them, against St. Paul; but of this there is no trace whatever. Bishop Westcott ranks Ebionism among the Christological errors which St. John meets (Epistles of St. John, p. xxxvi.). On the contention that at least some Pauline epistles exhibit a Christology too "advanced" to be really St. Paul's, cp. Hort, The Romans and the Ephesians, p. 123 ff.; and Knowling, The Witness of the Epistles, p. 256 ff., especially as to the significance of "the word Κύριος applied to Jesus" alike in "the earliest and the latest epistles."

the animating principles of Apostolic life, even more than any Apostolic utterances, bear witness to the Apostolic belief and teaching about the Saviour. It was transmitted to the sub-apostolic Church :[1] the earliest fathers do not all speak with the ringing emphasis of St. Ignatius about the identity of the Son of Mary with "our God,"[2] but, as Bishop Lightfoot has shown, they give no countenance to Humanitarianism, so called, in any shape. In fact, the strange popularity of Docetism involves a widespread belief in Divinity as attaching in some real sense to the Saviour :[3] what the Docetist mystics denied was just that bodily "reality" of His birth, His life on

[1] Such transmission would be independent of Scripture statements, but coincident with them.
[2] Ign. Eph. 18.
[3] The like may be said as to the spread of the theory broadly called Sabellian, an anticipation of which was known to Justin (Dial. 128). Praxeas and Noetus had a "zeal not according to knowledge" for the dignity of Our Lord when they identified Him with the Father.

earth, His death, His resurrection, on which Ignatius found it so specially necessary to insist.[1] When, about a century later, Gentile Humanitarians, followers of Theodotus of Byzantium in what a writer quoted by Eusebius[2] (with a special allusion to Theodotus' own case) brands as a "God-denying apostasy," pretended to represent the primeval belief of the Church, various great names were adduced in refutation:[3] yet

---

[1] Ign. Trall. 9; Smyrn. 1-3, 5. Cp. Tertull. de Carn. Chr. 5; adv. Marc. iii. 8.

[2] Euseb. v. 28. Salmon ascribes this "Little Labyrinth" to Caius, Dict. Chr. Biogr. iii. 98. Its writer alludes to the story afterwards given by Epiphanius, Hær. 54. 1, about Theodotus' "denial of Christ" in a persecution. If it is true, he must have first taken up a simply "Psilanthropist" view of Jesus Christ, and afterwards modified it by distinguishing in Cerinthian fashion between the man Jesus and a heavenly spirit called Christ, Refut. Hær. vii. 35. His original view was put into more definite form by Artemon, who regarded Jesus Christ as distinguished from prophets by (1) virgin-birth, (2) superior virtue (Theodoret, Hær. Fab. ii. 6).

[3] Justin, for one. His "mild judgment" as to "some" Humanitarian (or rather Psilanthropist) Christians was probably intended to assist Trypho towards

it might have sufficed (especially for Roman Christians) to utter the name of St. Paul. The legalist assailants of the "teacher of the Gentiles," who did their best to hunt him down and to blast his influence, were the precursors of those purely Judaic Ebionites, who gave distinct form to a vague "sentiment" of longstanding, an unwillingness to accept the idea of a really Divine Son of God.[1] Their abhorrence of Paul as a traitor to the Law was carried out into a positive denial of his Christology, which they easily learned to regard as idolatrous. And this denial was inherited by that later, more cultured, and more actively propagandist type of Ebionism in which Essene and quasi-Gnostic elements seems to have met,[2] and

a recognition of Jesus as the Christ (Dial. 48). On the orthodoxy of the "thorough Hebrew" Hegesippus, cp. Lightfoot, Dissert., p. 89.

[1] Cp. Lightfoot, Dissert. p. 78.

[2] Lightfoot, *l.c.* In this strange Christology Adam is the first, and Jesus the last, of the men in or by whom a super-angelic "Christ," or created "Son," became manifest as "the True Prophet."

which effloresced in that Pseudo-Clementine literature wherein a destructive heresy was popularised by a coating of biographical romance.

The form which the Christology of the typical Apostles assumed in the second century was, and indeed could not but be, unsystematic: it might be condensed into summary statements[1] which one might call primitive creeds, and of which we find germs in the New Testament; but the time was not come for dealing with the task of combining theoretically the inviolable first principle of the Divine Unity with the Christian conception of a Son of God whose sonship, being unique, involved an identity of nature or "essence" with that "Father," in whom the idea of Divine Unity was for the earliest believers specially concentrated,[2]

---

[1] Cp. Irenæus, i. 10. 1, and Tertull. Præscr. Hær. 13; ad Prax. 2.

[2] When Tertullian wrote against Praxeas, the majority of African Christians, through want of instruction, thought

although their successors, through further meditation on the doctrine of the Trinity

the doctrine of the Trinity inconsistent with what was called the " Monarchia." Thus " Monarchianism " could take two heretical forms—the Sabellian and the " Psilanthropist." Yet all, however "simple," who worshipped Christ, implicitly admitted the Divinity of the Son. And the only theologian among primitive Roman bishops speaks of the Trinity as " recapitulated into " the Father, because the Divinity of the Son and the Spirit depends on Their relation to the Father (Dion. Rom. ap. Routh, Rell. Sacr. iii. 374). Cp. the first part of the Te Deum, and the ordinary " preface," as followed by the Tersanctus, in our liturgy. As for Tertullian's own Christology, Dorner says that by associating the Son overmuch with the formation of the finite world, he was led to " subordinate " the Son to a degree inconsistent with his own general view of the actual God as having come near to us in Christ; but, as " an Arian subordinationism was foreign to his mind, he would not purchase the Divine Unity at that price." He reconciled it with personal distinctions by asserting the consubstantiality and recognising the coinherence; but inasmuch as he made the Sonship begin with the act of creation, his hold on Trinitarian doctrine was defective. Newman says that his " denial of Our Lord's eternity as the Son " does not prove " that he denied the eternity of His *hypostasis* as the Word;" and although " to suppose the *genesis* to be a divine act, not in eternity, but in time, is an offence not only against the perfection of the Triad, but primarily against the simplicity and unchangeableness of the Divine Monad," and its contents, associated that idea (as we find it in the *Quicunque*) rather with the one "Godhead" existing in "Three Persons." But the New Testament had passages which showed that the combination referred to must be made, if Christianity were to be understood and mentally grasped, to reign in the thoughts as well as in the affections: and the crude, or one-sided, or otherwise unsatisfactory language, which is to be found in the writings of various Christian divines before the Nicene Council,[1] is only an

---

yet "much may be said in his excuse. His religious knowledge was not ours; truths are taken for granted now on all hands which had to be learned one by one then," etc. (Tracts Theol. and Eccles. pp. 187, 189). By "truths" should here be understood necessary inferences from the two great *credenda*, the Divine Unity and the personal Divine Sonship.

[1] *E.g.* the language which exaggerates the "Subordinatio Filii," or which treats the Filiation as an event in time (see Newman, Tracts Theol. and Eccles. p. 126 ff.). In Hermas (Sim. v.) the confusion of language is remarkable. In his parable of the vineyard, the faithful slave of the owner is distinguished from his "son," and made "co-heir" with him. But in the explanation, in order to

illustration of the difficulties of the task of finding accurate terms for a subject so mysterious, and of doing justice to both aspects of the problem. Yet all the while the Church lived on and by the assurance that God was veritably One, and that yet He had a real Son who was as veritably Divine, and a Spirit who, as we should now put it, was both Divine and personal: and the development ultimately given, after much debate, and much experience of untenable theories, "did but put into dogmatic language, according to the best methods then accessible," the idea which alone could truly represent the mind of St. Paul or of St. John, and

avoid a seeming disparagement of Christ, the slave himself is called God's Son, and the proper heir is called the Holy Spirit; what is meant being the glorification of Christ's manhood or flesh as united with His Person or His Godhead, called the Son, and also Holy Spirit (cp. Heb. ix. 14). This is a very untheological way of speaking; but no Ebionite would have employed it (see Pullan, Hist. of Early Christianity, p. 141; cp. also Herm. Sim. ix. 12. 2, "The Son is older than all His creation").

which had been the inspiring and sustaining force at work in primitive sanctity, primitive devotion, and primitive martyrdom. For the primitive Church would not have been what she was, if she had not had a Christ to adore.

(4.)

This brings us to consider the type of character which, on the whole, distinguished the Church of the earliest centuries. It was, we have seen, the outcome of faith in a "supernatural" and Divine Christ; the memory of a naturalistic Christ, or even of an Ebionitish Christ distinguished from other men by superior moral "attainment,"[1] could never have sufficed for such results; and

---

[1] Eusebius applies the phrase προκοπὴν ἤθους (usually associated with the theory of Paul of Samosata) in this connection (iii. 27). Both he and Origen say that even those Ebionites who acknowledged the Virgin-birth (and who are often identified with the Nazarenes) denied the personal divinity of Jesus (Orig. in Matt. xvi. 12).

those who say that a simply human teacher was gradually sublimated into a God incarnate by the mere working of an idolatrous enthusiasm—for the supposition carries with it a charge of virtual idolatry—are in effect saying that the moral transformation which that early Christianity wrought on so many who adopted it was due to an illusion, not only enormous, but pernicious; for what could be more pernicious than that hundreds of converts should mistake a fellow-man pure and simple for their God? In a measure, the primitive Church could say that its "life in the flesh was lived in the faith of the Son of God:" but as, even in Pauline days, and notably at Corinth, tares grew up with the wheat,—as Churches within reach of St. John's own presence could "leave their first love," could be tolerant of gross evils, or complacently lukewarm, or chilled with the beginnings of spiritual deadness,—so it was in the sub-apostolic age, when Clement had to rebuke a "hateful sedition," or Polycarp to lament the misconduct of a presbyter;[1] or perhaps later, when Hermas (*if* we take the usually received and later date of his writing) found reason to utter his symbolic warnings against unreal or superficial conversion, or absorption in "much business," or contentiousness, or self-indulgence requiring "punishment;"[2] or when Tertullian met the pagan taunt about the bad lives of some Christians by observing that it implicitly acknowledged the high moral standard involved in Christianity.[3] It was only too easy, one finds, for Christians even then to be "conformed to the age" in

---

[1] Valens. Lightfoot thinks his fault was avarice. As for crimes, Tertullian appeals to the records of trials in proof that no one condemned as an assassin or a robber has been also set down as a Christian (Apol. 44).

[2] Cp. Sim. viii. 9. 1; 13. 2; iv. 5; ix. 20. 1; viii. 7. 4; vi. 3. 3. He is also severe on "men of two souls," who halt between belief and unbelief.

[3] Ad. Nat. i. 5. He adds, "But you have no right to call them Christians to whom Christians deny that name."

the sense deprecated by the Apostle of the Gentiles,—only too easy to forget the need of moral vigilance amid the influences of "heathen friendships;"[1] and we have a vivid condensed picture, in the next century, of "the cankers of a calm world and a long peace," as apparent in the comfortable worldliness, not only of laymen, but of priests and even of bishops, immersed in gainful pursuits throughout the north-west of Africa.[2]

---

[1] Hermas, Mand. x. 1. 4.

[2] See the famous passage, so piercing in its detailed censures, in Cypr. de Lapsis, 6, where he speaks of bishops who had actually "deserted their chairs in order to pursue gain in foreign markets." As Newman points out, this would diminish conversions, and stop the advance of the Church (Callista, p. 15). Origen not only says, "We have learned not to relax our vigilance in time of peace, and give ourselves up to repose," but refers to some priests and prelates who "came very far short of their duty, and lived more indolently than those who were of firmer tone" (c. Cels. iii. 15, 30). So Commodianus, in one of his strange rough verses: "Sub pace ... de vobis vix unus caute se gerit." Eusebius begins his account of the Diocletian persecution by saying that the previous "liberty" had produced first "empty-headed sluggishness," and then a bitter contentiousness even among clergy (viii. 1).

But the Church had also to deal with misdeeds which compromised her purity.

The treatment of grievous offences had been provided for by the commission given to the Apostles to retain as well as to remit sins; and we have at least one example of the exercise of this jurisdiction in the apostolical period. The instance of the incestuous Corinthian, already referred to, shows that the decisive judgment rested with Apostles, although they might delegate the power of pronouncing it in their own behalf to a local Church which would doubtless act by its officials, and might thus take pains to secure the Church's moral support in the carrying out of a spiritual discipline, which had for its object the reformation and salvation of the sinner, and the absence of which among "heretics" was noted as a bad moral sign.[1] When he

[1] Hermas may perhaps be alluding to such a discipline in Vis. iii. 7; but he regards all sin as capable

showed repentance, the censure was to be taken off; but as cases of grave sin multi-

of Divine forgiveness if repented of. Dionysius of Corinth, in 169, advised the churches of Pontus to receive back, on repentance, all who had been excommunicated for "any kind" of sin (Euseb. iv. 23). But at Rome the discipline of the second century was sterner: idolatry, murder, or unchastity involved perpetual exclusion from Roman Church-fellowship, until Zephyrinus, to the disgust of Tertullian (de Pudic. 1), modified the rule in regard to the last of these three sins. Callistus went further, and allowed penance, followed by absolution, to Christians guilty of the two former offences,—thus, as Döllinger says, clearing his church's method from the charge of inconsistency. But some African bishops disapproved even of Zephyrinus' relaxation of the old rigour (cp. Cypr. Ep. 55. 21). Tertullian, as a Catholic, says that the "heretics" had no discipline; they thought it inconsistent with "simplicity," and ascribed the Church's solicitude about it to a "corrupt taste," *i.e.* for forms and externalism (De Præscr. Hær. 41. Origen had at one time denied that a bishop could absolve those who had committed any of the three great sins (de Orat. 28); but later he only says (c. Cels. iv. 27, iii. 51) that evil-doers among Christians can hardly escape detection, which would involve "exclusion from the common prayers" (a general term for the Eucharistic service); that they are not restored on proof of repentance without a longer probation than is required before baptism; and that they are not thereafter admissible to any office of rule in the Church.

plied, it became necessary, in the words of our Commination Service, to "put" the repentant offender to "open penance," which Irenæus first, and after him Tertullian, call by the emphatic term *exomologesis*.[1] It was ordinarily a course of public self-humiliation, accompanied by fastings and prayer, and entreaties for the intercession of the clergy and the faithful, or, as Tertullian calls them, "the beloved of God;" and it involved a temporary exclusion from Church-privileges,[2] together

---

[1] Tertull. de Pœnit. 9: cp. Euseb. v. 28. Cyprian adopts the term from his "teacher," and says that it involved a careful scrutiny of the conduct of the professing penitent (Ep. 17. 2: cp. Ep. 15. 1; 16. 2; 20. 3). When it had been gone through to the satisfaction of the bishop and the presbyters, the penitent was restored to communion by the imposition of their hands. But there was also private confession, made either (1) in serious illness (Cypr. Ep. 18. 1), or (2) for advice as to whether public confession was needful (Orig. in Ps. 37, h. 2).

[2] See the tale (given as such in Euseb. vi. 34) of the Emperor Philip being ordered by St. Babylas "to make confession, and to take his place among those who were reckoned as transgressors, and who had a place

with a graduated scale of spiritual penalties, in accordance with the differing qualities of the sins which had scandalised the Church, and a corresponding classification—more complete, it seems, in the East than in the West—of the persons undergoing the process of discipline.[1]

Let all dreamings about a purely golden age of the Church be known for what they are—fancies that waste thought and ensure disappointment; but after all due allowance for the extent to which, even while Apostles lived, and still more after the memory of their work had become a tradition, Christian profession was contradicted by Christian misconduct, there can be no doubt that a vast moral force was set at work which

---

of repentance." On the minor excommunication for offences less heinous than the "capital" sins, *e.g.* for fraudulent detention of property, cp. Bingham, xvi. 2. 7.

[1] The mourners, hearers, kneelers, and "co-standers;" this last class were allowed to attend the whole Eucharistic service, but not to communicate.

braced, deepened, and consolidated the characters of those who came vitally into contact with it. To adopt a single sentence of Mr. Lecky's—" Noble lives, crowned by heroic deaths, were the best arguments of the infant Church."[1] Justin, who had gone through several schools of philosophy in his search for the goodly pearl of truth, testifies, as one who knew, that the adoption of the faith had actually turned men from evil to good; profligates had become pure; some who once made wealth their object now shared what they possessed with "every one in need;" and the bitter hatred which raged between men of different nationalities had been superseded by practical "philanthropy."[2] Here were *facts;* and so Clement

---

[1] Hist. Europ. Morals, i. 441.
[2] Apol. i. 14, 65; ii. 2. Cp. St. Athanasius, de Incarn. Verbi, 51. Origen dwells on the "philanthropy of the (Christian) doctrine" (c. Cels. i. 27; cp. ib. iv. 28). So the Epistle to Diognetus, 5: "Christians love all men." On the last point, cp. Tyrwhitt's Greek and Gothic, p. 140, that the "ancient catacomb paintings

of Alexandria commences his singular anapæstic "Hymn to the Saviour" by invoking Him as "bridle of colts untamed;" and elsewhere asserts that the "new song" of Divine truth in the Word has given life to some that were morally "dead;"—that men have become better parents, husbands, masters, for accepting and assimilating Christianity; and that one result of Christ's "tuition" is "a generous disposition corresponding to a purpose formed by the love of what is excellent."[1] Tertullian complains of the perversity of those pagans who were irritated even by undeniable moral improvement when produced by conversion to the faith; but he also knows of happier cases, in which a converted wife has become so manifestly a

made men feel that Christ was the Shepherd of men," that in Him senators and "the Davuses of the slave-market" were alike one.

[1] Cohort. 4, 107; Pædag. i. 99. So he says characteristically, "The Saviour has many tones in His voice, and is versatile" (the Odyssean πολύτροπος) "in working out the salvation of men" (Cohort. 8; cp. Pæd. i. 75).

"better woman," that her pagan husband, convinced by a genuine "experience," has himself followed her example.[1] And the great Origen, who had had signal opportunities of estimating the effects of Christian belief on conduct, challenges unbelievers who call it "pernicious" to explain the fact that many who once were "licentious, unjust, or covetous," are now known in their new character as Christians to be "more equitable, more serious, more steadfast," or consistent; he dwells on "the true manliness of a Christian life," exhibited in "that splendid quality of justice which makes human fellowship a reality, and preserves fairness, philanthropy, and kindness,"—and again remarks that Christians refrain from that "servile flattery of princes, which is unworthy of brave and high-minded men."[2] What is

---

[1] Tertull. Apol. 3, and ad Ux. ii. 7.
[2] Orig. c. Cels. i. 26; iv. 26; viii. 65. So Aznobius says that in the Church service nothing is heard "nisi

this but to testify that characters, when touched by Christ, had not been weakened but strengthened; that the faith had acted on them like a tonic, had made them more effectively *human*? And there is much significance in the epithets which the father of ecclesiastical history in the next century applies to the type of thought and action which prevailed within the "Catholic and only true Church;" he calls it "serious, sincere, free-spirited, self-controlled, and pure."[1] The word which I have rendered "serious," and which, in one form or other, is familiar to the readers of St. Paul, is properly associated with the idea of dignity or grandeur.[2] As used in regard to the early Christians, it tells us that amid a world which was frivolous because hopeless, they were grave because

quod humanos faciat . . . mites, verecundos, pudicos, castos, familiaris communicatores rei" (iv. 36).

[1] Euseb. iv. 7.

[2] Cp. Tertull. de Præscr. Hær. 43, "gravitas honesta." This is just the σεμνότης of 1 Tim. ii. 2.

they reverenced their own high calling as Christians, and looked at all things in the light of it; and yet, with all their habitual recollectedness, with an intense conviction of the solemnity of life, of the awfulness of its issues, of the deep-seated malignity of sin,[1] of the close observant nearness of God as Judge, these spiritual ancestors of ours had found the secret of being permanently happy;[2] life, for them, had a real brightness; amid a world full of hostile forces, and prospects appalling to flesh and blood, they had "made their souls their own in their patience,"[3] and looked forward with glad confidence to the consummation of that "peace" which already they felt to be such a gift as the world could neither give nor take away. Thus one of their writers could say of them

[1] "With us, even a sinful thought is a sin" Minucius Felix, Octav. 35.
[2] "Exultant because of their faith" (Clem. Alex. Pædag. i. 15).
[3] Luke xxi. 19.

what was eminently true of himself, that they "were always young."[1] Dean Church, whose words are never unmeasured, speaks of their souls as filled with "an awful rejoicing transport" by the assurance that "the visitation and presence of Divine and unearthly Goodness in human form" had brought with it "a new and astonishing possibility, that goodness" was really attainable for "men not here and there, but on a large scale,—within the reach of those who seemed most beyond it."[2] The life of Christ had set up a moral ideal which Christians really tried to aim at, which was " mirrored more or

---

[1] Clem. Alex. Pædag. i. 20.

[2] Gifts of Civilisation, etc., pp. 183–185. So Tyrwhitt, Greek and Gothic, p. 145: "In primitive days people seem honestly to have looked over and beyond death.... They dwelt on the Lord's victory rather than on His sufferings." They did not mind borrowing from secular art the form of a youthful shepherd to represent the "Pastor bonus," especially as this would "present the Redeemer to neophytes in a type familiar and pleasing to the Roman eye" (Lanciani, Pag. and Chr. Rome, p. 348). Of course this was "looking at one side."

less perfectly in a thousand lives;" and they believed that He was not only their exemplar of virtue, but their moral Re-creator as well. As Cardinal Newman puts it, in words which, once read, are not soon forgotten,[1] it was "the thought, or image, or idea of Christ, imprinted by Himself in the minds of His subjects individually," and producing a "sovereign devotion to an invisible Lord," which made it natural for Origen to begin his great work in support of Christianity with such calmly majestic assurance; "It is by the lives of His genuine disciples that Jesus even now makes His defence." It was this which produced a new development of veracity, as binding a man to be faithful to conviction at any cost, while it made him scorn the trickeries and falsities of Greek speech.[2] It was this which, as we

[1] Grammar of Assent, p. 458 ff. Of Gibbon's "causes" he asks, "Why did he not try the hypothesis of faith, hope, and charity?" (ib. p. 456).

[2] Cp. Justin, Apol. ii. 2; Tatian, ad Græcos, 32,

now express it, brought religion into everyday life, into the business of the shop or the market.¹ It was this which enabled Tertullian, with all his strong feeling in favour of celibacy, to draw his beautiful sketch of the happiness of Christian married life,² wherein husband and wife are "together in prayer, in church, at God's feast, in persecutions, in times of repose." It was this which kindled a passion of active charity towards the brethren, and towards all suf-

"When we speak we utter no falsehood:" so Hermas, Mand. iii. 2, "Those who lie ignore the Lord:" and Origen, c. Cels. vii. 66, on the immorality of insincere compliance with idolatry.

¹ So Clem. Alex., Cohort. 100, that husbandmen, sailors, soldiers, can, as such, serve God; and (Pædag. iii. 78) that a Christian can do his worldly business κατὰ Θεόν, e.g. he will not name two prices in buying or selling.

² "Quod ecclesia conciliat, et confirmat oblatio, et obsignat benedictio, angeli renuntiant, Pater rato habet," ad Uxor. ii. 9. Cp. Clem. Alex. Pædag. i. 10; "Both have one God, one Guide, one Church . . . a marriage of equal yoke . . . grace, salvation, love, and mode of life in common."

ferers as such, known or unknown, distant or at hand;[1] which made the Agape and the collection for the poor to be genuine expressions of brotherly sympathy, and the service of God in Christ to be very effectually a service of man;[2] which sanctified what Origen nobly calls "that splendid quality of justice, which preserves what is social and just, and philanthropic and kind, in our relations with neighbours and kindred;"[3] which utilised a terrible pestilence for the exhibition of a contrast between cowardly heathen selfishness and the "sublime charity" of Christian

[1] Cp. Justin Martyr, Apol. i. 67: Dionysius of Corinth in Euseb. iv. 23; and Tertullian, Apol. 39.

[2] The "leaven" deposited by the Christian idea of God and of man was fully at work when Christians were exhorted to treat their bond-servants as themselves; "for to the free and to the slaves, God is, *if you consider*, ἴσος" (Clem. Alex. Pæd. iii. 92; cp. Cyprian, ad Dem. 8).

[3] Orig. c. Cels. iv. 26. Lucian remarks that Christians "spare no expense" in assisting their imprisoned co-religionists, for "their first legislator had persuaded them to believe that they were all brethren of each other" (De Morte Peregrini, 13).

self-devotion.[1] It was this which confronted the insolent foulness of pagan vice by a burning enthusiasm for purity, and an equable antagonism to all forms of moral mischief, such as was embodied in that "sacred pledge"[2] to eschew evil, which formed part of the "antelucan" worship of the Bithynian Christians, when a fair-minded provincial governor made official inquiry into their habits,—and which virtually involved a renewal of the baptismal vow of "renunciation." And surely it was this which for them made life worth living, and caused their "joy," as a fruit of the Spirit, to contrast so enviably with the "disgust and sated loathing," which, in Matthew Arnold's

---

[1] Cp. Dion. Alex. in Euseb. vii. 22, on the tender ministrations in which not a few lost their lives; and Pontius, Life of Cyprian, 10, on the business-like arrangements which brought relief to Christians and heathens alike (cp. also Cypr. de Mortal. 16).

[2] There can surely be no doubt that this is the sense of "sacramentum" in Pliny's letter; but, of course, such a pledge would naturally link itself to Holy Communion.

wonderful picture of a Roman patrician's attempts to escape from himself, had "fallen" on a "pagan world" at once brutally "hard" and radically corrupt.[1] That "Babylon" was too far diseased to be "healed;"[2] but in some of her districts, and in many of her cities,[3] in "*the* City" itself, among the crowded dwellings of its poor,[4] under the "golden roofs" of a few of its proud families, in the quiet "houses" of a Prisca or a Pudens,[5] in the quarters of court

---

[1] "Obermann once more." Cp. Döllinger, Gentile and Jew, ii. 288: "Under the empire" the notion "of the emptiness of existence became more frequent," etc. (cp. Dean Farrar, Seekers after God, p. 49).

[2] Jer. li. 9.

[3] For Edessa, cp. Westcott on Canon, p. 239; for Eumeneia, Ramsay, Cit. and Bish. of Phrygia, ii. 502.

[4] In the Suburra and the Velabrum (cp. Merivale, Hist. Rome. vi. 355); the "patrician mansions" were on the hills or their slopes. The house of Glabrio covered a great space on the Pincian.

[5] The "house of Prisca" was in the seclusion of the Aventine; that of Pudens on "the southern slope of the Viminal" (Tyrwhitt, Greek and Gothic, p. 88; Lanciani, Pag. and Chr. Rome, p. 110). Naturally, as we know from Rom. xvi. 5 (cp. Col. iv. 15), the "house" of Aquila

pages[1] or other servants of emperors on the Palatine, "the Lord had much people;" the leaven had got a long way into the lump when the Constantinian period opened; or, to vary the image from the story of the most benign of prophets, there were tokens enough of the healing energy of that Presence which had come into men's lives as "a new cruse with salt therein."

and Priscilla was used for Christian worship. So the wealthy believers would open their ample halls to their fellow-Christians for a like purpose. These domestic churches were the prototypes of the basilicas.

[1] The Domus Gelotiana on the south side of the imperial hill, where Alexamenos and his "God" were caricatured, and Libanus, perhaps, was nicknamed "the bishop" (Lanciani, p. 12). Irenæus refers to (adult) Christians "in regali aula," who contributed to the needs of their poorer brethren (iv. 30. 1).

ADDRESS IV.

It may be asked why a faith which showed so much power, not only to diffuse and sustain a worthy conception of Deity, but to promote moral and social good, to recall men from manifold debasements to righteousness, humanity, and cleanness of life, to exhibit a pattern of internal unity wherein authority and liberty were combined, was not more readily welcomed, and had such uphill work in making its way. Those who now treat it as discredited by its "supernaturalism" are fond of ascribing such acceptance as it met with in the second century, for instance, to the eagerness of men in that age, amid the thickening distresses and perils of the empire, for glimpses into the unseen world. This, it is urged, made them greedy of mere "wonders;" and thus the Christian "legend" got a hearing from the credulous—the rather that it found its first converts, as a rule, not among the cultured classes, which were "honeycombed" with philosophical scepticism,[1] but rather, as its great Apostle acknowledged, or even boasted, among the "weak" and the despised of this world. But there is supernaturalism *and* supernaturalism. Did the conditions of social life prepare the average subject of Cæsar for *such* a "miraculous religion" as Christianity? Whether we look at auguries and omens, and the paraphernalia of the official "cult,"[2] or at the worship of Æsculapius revived in a period of epidemics, and

---

[1] Juvenal must have had some sort of warrant for saying that "even boys no longer believed" in the stories about the world of the dead (Sat. ii. 149).

[2] On the established and familiar supernaturalism of the Roman state religion, cp. Gladstone, Gleanings, viii. 95.

the oracles of such a charlatan as Alexander of Abonoteichos, whom even Marcus Aurelius "took seriously,"[1] and the juggleries of wizards, and the revolting lustrations of the worship of Cybele,[2] what pressure did any of these put upon conduct? What resemblance did they bear to that belief in the Crucified and Risen, which brought with it the demand for a complete moral self-surrender? This demand ran clean athwart the ingrained traditional ideas of those who would never omit a prescribed ceremonial connected with pagan altars, or who rushed in terror or in anxiety to a pagan hierophant or a

[1] Allard, Hist. des Perséc. i. 338. On this impostor cp. Döllinger, Gentile and Jew, etc., ii. 198. Lightfoot says, "The rising tide of this pagan reaction brought in on its surface from far and wide the refuse of the basest superstitions and impostures" (SS. Ignat. and Polycarp, i. 450).

[2] Döllinger says, "The first instance of a taurobolium, as far as is known, occurred in the year A.D. 133," and was connected with the worship of the Carthaginian Queen of Heaven, "by this time identified with Cybele" (Gentile and Jew, etc. ii. 108).

travelling soothsayer, or to one of those astrologers whom the Romans called "mathematici."[1] Or even supposing that there was no reluctance to submit to ethical restraints, the example of Julian in a later age shows clearly enough that men could reject the supernaturalism of the Gospel and the Church just because it was too austere, too reserved, too unsensational, too glaringly

[1] "The people were smitten with an access of superstitious devotion . . . they raised new shrines to every deity whose power might temper for their preservation . . . the air and the water" (cp. Merivale, Hist. of Rom. under the Empire, viii. 360). In all this there was no craving for *spiritual* help; the hunger was not for "the food that endureth" (John vi. 27). "La réaction païenne," says De Pressensé, "partit d'en bas et non d'en haut; elle fut éminemment populaire;" . . . "la recrudescence de ce paganisme aussi fanatique que *démoralisé*" (Trois Prem. Siècl. 2me série, ii. 3, 33). Even when imperial patronage favoured the attempt to set up Apollonius as the rival Christ of Neoplatonism, he had to be adapted to the taste of a generation fascinated by the pretensions of magic. No wonder, then, that Macrianus, whom Dionysius of Alexandria calls "chief of the synagogue of Egyptian magicians" (Euseb. vii. 10), urged Valerian, at first tolerant, to become a persecutor.

unlike what they craved for, what alone they could appreciate, what they found in current thaumaturgy. It was not, then, by its affirmations about a God incarnate, or by reports of miraculous powers attaching to its representatives, that Christianity could win favour from the multitude. Rather was this multitude predisposed against a faith which, if adopted, would deprive them of so much that, in their view, was indispensable to their enjoyment. Its talk about Christ as a deliverer from sin would appeal to nothing in their souls; they had yet to learn what sin meant.[1] They had no taste, or rather they had a rooted distaste, for a religion which, being real, was moral. Here, then, we come to the first point in the consideration of the Church's position with reference to the heathen world outside. What was her relation to its society?

[1] Even Mithraism, with its severe probations and its promise of victory over death, did not come near Christianity in this respect.

(1.)

To begin with, idolatry in its many forms, antique or novel, magnificent or fantastic, was ubiquitous and supreme. It stared a Christian in the face at every turn.[1] He could not walk the streets of his own town, nor go into fields or gardens outside it, nor pass through the vestibule of a house,[2] nor look at the exterior ornaments of a temple, without being challenged by the symbols,

---

[1] Cp. Tertull. de Spectac. 8, "Streets, and forum, and baths, and inns, and our very houses, sine idolis omnino non sunt:" and de Idol. 16, "Ita *Malus* circumdedit sæculum idololatriâ." Hence the need of habitual caution. "Amid these rocks and creeks, and shoals and straits, of idolatry, faith, wafted on by the Spirit of God, makes her voyage—tuta si cauta, secura si attonita," ib. 24. "At every step which a Greek or Roman took, he was confronted by images of his gods and memorials of their mythic history. Not the temples only, but streets and public squares, house-walls, domestic implements, and drinking-vessels were all covered with ornaments of this kind" (Döllinger, Gentile and Jew, etc., ii. 196).

[2] Cp. Tertull. de Idol. 15, on the gods of doors and thresholds.

too often demoralising or abominable, of its presence and its dominion;[1] and even where morality was not outraged, the glorious beauty of temples and images might have for weaker souls the fascination of a Siren-song; and this explains the disposition of austere Christian teachers to keep art, as such, at arm's length.[2] Such notions as we can form of this daily experience may help us to understand why an early Christian was taught and accustomed to guard imagination and sanctify memory, "at his going out and coming in," and in all the movements of life, by "marking his forehead with the sign of the Cross."[3] There was often a difficulty for him in the pursuit of a business or profession; some could be pursued without risk

---

[1] This is vividly set forth in the tenth chapter of Cardinal Newman's "Callista."

[2] "How little would Christian or heathen have presaged that art was not to perish, but only to be redeemed!" Trench, Huls. Lect. p. 122.

[3] Tertull. de Cor. 3.　Cp. ad Ux. ii. 9.

to the conscience, and we know that Christians did carry on trades, and made profit by them;[1] but on others the trail of the serpent was only too visible. A Christian sculptor, for instance, might any day be called upon to carve the figure of a pagan god. He must not salve his conscience by saying that "to make it was not to worship it," or that "a man must live, and that was *his* livelihood."[2] He must simply refuse, at any cost, to " make an idol "—let him "polish a slab" instead ;[3] but this would attract the hostile observation of men like those who made "silver shrines of Artemis." It was embarrassing to keep a school ;[4] pagan fables

---

[1] Irenæus, iv. 30. 1.

[2] Tertull. de Idol. 5, 6, 12.

[3] Ib. 8. He reminds Christians that if crafts which "ensure a livelihood without transgression of Christian duty" do not pay so well, they give "more constant employment."

[4] Ib. 10. Here the danger was much greater for the teacher than for the scholar (ib.). The great rigorist, who scented idolatry almost everywhere, admits

were mixed up with common literature; fees and presents were associated with pagan festivals of Minerva, of Flora, or of the Seven Hills of Rome. If a Christian of the upper class became a magistrate, questions of conscience at once beset him; large parts of his official duty must be left undone, because they involved compliance with idolatry.[1] Military service involved at least some difficulty of this sort;[2] and as for the "pleasures" or "sports" which were so

---

that some family observances, such as that of putting on the dress of the adult, or even espousals, need not be avoided; if one has to attend them on such an occasion, and will not be compromised by any apparent participation in a sacrifice, let people do as they like (ib. 16). So he admits that one must often name an idol, as when saying, "I live in Isis Street," or, "You will find him in Æsculapius' temple" (ib. 20). Similarly in De Cor. 8, he freely allows the use of things which procure "meras utilitates, et certa subsidia, et honesta solatia," for the needs of human life.

[1] De Idol. 17. But he also thinks any infliction of judicial punishment a task unfit for Christians.

[2] Cp. the distinction between joining and remaining in the army, Tert. de Cor. 11.

popular that the suspension of them might provoke a riot, it might be pleaded that intrinsically they were but opportunities for admiration of God's own creatures, of the speed of the horse, or the melody of the voice: but abuse, it was replied,[1] had become absolutely inseparable from use; the "shows" were named after idols, images were borne in procession before their commencement, the figure of the Sun-god predominated over the circus; and further, the games were scenes of maddening excitement,[2] the gladiatorial exhibitions were a school of ferocity,[3] and in theatres one could not but hear what

[1] Tertull. de Spectaculis, 2.

[2] "'Madness' became a technical term in designating the circus" (Pusey, note to Tertull. de Spect. 16. Lib. Fath. Cp. Minucius Felix, Octavius, 37, "populi in se rixantis insaniam;" and Juvenal, xi. 196 ff.

[3] "We think that to look on a homicide is as bad as to perpetrate it" (Athenag. Legat. 35. So Theophilus, iii. 15). "Si sævitiam . . . si impietatem, si feritatem, permissam nobis contendere possumus, eamus in amphitheatrum" (Tertull. de Spect. 19); "In ludis . . . gladiatoriis homicidii *disciplinam*" (Minuc. Felix, Octavius, 37). Cp. Gibbon, iv. 40 (c. 30).

for a Christian it was "a shame to speak of,"[1] —to such a pass had come that animalism which modern "Hellenists" have sometimes dared to regret, as a brightness too long driven out of life by the "pale shadow of the Galilæan.' If a Christian of the shop-keeping class, or one poorer yet and lower in standing, made a conscience of keeping aloof from these degrading amusements, he would of course encounter sneers and growls as a "surly kill-joy."[2] The high-born Christian could avoid such insults: he could shut himself up for the day in his stately house,[3]

---

[1] Cp. the story in Tertull. de Spect. 26 ("In meo eam inveni"). The profligacy of the theatres long survived the (so-called) triumph of Christianity, and stirred the indignation of St. Chrysostom at the Easter of 399.

[2] So the Epistle to Diognetus, c. 6: "The world hates the Christians because they set themselves against pleasures." And the pagan says in Octavius, 12, "Honestis voluptatibus abstinetis," etc. This abstinence, felt as a rebuke, was irritating.

[3] On the number of high-born Roman converts in the early Christian period, such as Flavius Clemens the

but he would know well enough that his neighbours, patrician or plebeian, were calling him first morose and unsocial, "of no good to any one in matters of daily life,"[1] and then, by rapid but not unnatural inference, "*uncivic*, — alien from Roman ways, — indeed, most likely, dangerous to Roman interests, disloyal to the State and the emperor."[2] Such murmurs, he would be

---

consul, Domitian's cousin, and his wife Flavia Domitilla, Domitian's niece,—Pomponia Græcina,—and Acilius Glabrio: cp. Lightfoot's St. Clement, i. 19, 30 ff.; Ramsay, The Church in R. Empire, p. 260; and Lanciani, Pag. and Chr. Rome, pp. 3–10. On the catacomb of Domitilla, ib. pp. 335–342; and Lightfoot, i. 35 ff.; and on that of Priscilla in the Via Salaria, Lanciani, pp. 7, 111. That of Callistus was given by a noble Christian family. Eusebius (v. 21) mentions the martyrdom of Apollonius, whom Jerome calls a senator (De Vir. Illustr. 42).

[1] "Infructuosi," Tertull. Apol. 42. Cp. the charge of "inertia," Suet., Dom. 15. "The Church in Asia Minor" set herself to refute it;" cp. Ramsay, p. 435.

[2] Tertullian replies at length to the charge of belonging to "an unlawful faction" (Apol. 38). But in that very chapter he gives occasion for suspicion by saying, "Nobis . . . nec ulla magis res aliena quam publica;

well aware, might at no distant time be translated into active hostility. The state of tension in which a true-hearted Christian had to live would make his Lord's admonition "to all" unspeakably significant; he must be ever "on the watch" against temptations to compromise his fidelity, to think that "he might just as well, for once in a way, conform to what everybody did—that to him it would really mean nothing, while to make himself peculiar by a stiff noncompliance would only bring fresh odium on his religion, and forfeit influence which he might be able to use for good,[1]—and that, of course, he could stop at any point whenever he chose." He would know of many who

unam omnium rempublicam agnoscimus—*mundum*." So the writer to Diognetus, c. 5: "Every foreign country is to them a native country, and every native country is foreign." One can imagine a pagan reader's comment: "This is just what we say of you,—you don't care for *Rome*. She is no more to you than the barbarians beyond the frontier."

[1] Tertull. de Idol. 14; de Cult. Fæm. ii. 11.

had glided into a position neither avowed Christian nor actually pagan, who allied themselves with pagan families, adopted pagan forms of speech, and kept their Christian belief as "a thing between themselves and God."[1] Such a condition of mind would find out those who acquiesced in it, whenever the mob took up the cry which, we are told, was often heard when drought or famine, pestilence or earthquake, were interpreted as the vengeance of the gods on an empire that allowed the "atheists" to increase with such alarming rapidity; "To the lion with the Christians!"[2] At such moments

---

[1] Some such compromise is implied, if not in the appearance of winged genii in the earliest class of Christian paintings (Roma Sotterranea, p. 73), at any rate in the occasional intrusion of D.M. or "Diis Manibus" into inscriptions on Christian tombs; cp. Merivale, Hist. Rom. vi. 444; Dict. Chr. Antiq. i. 851.

[2] The classical passage is Tertull. Apol. 40. The shout, he says, is "still heard in every popular gathering" (de Res. Carn. 22; cf. de Spectac. 26, ad Nat. i. 1). Cyprian—against whom it had often been raised (Ep. 59. 6)—knew that pagans "imputed to Christians the

of furious panic, those hideous fictions which the savage or sensual fancy of slaves had fashioned out of conversations overheard,[1] or which, as Justin says, even relatives had repeated under torture,[2] or had invented under pressure, would acquire a fresh credibility, or rather, would be eagerly caught up.[3] To take the two

prevalence of war, pestilence, famine," etc. (Ad Demetr. 2). Cp. Arnobius, adv. Gent. i. 3 (adding "locusts").

[1] Tertull. ad Nat. i. 7 : "domesticorum curiositas," etc. He asks, of what value is such information? The writers of the Epistle of the churches of Vienne and Lyons say, "Some household servants, in fear of torture, and under the prompting of soldiers, told these lies against us" (Euseb. v. 1. 12; cf. Irenæan Fragments, No. 13). Athenagoras, very shortly before, says point-blank that "no slave ever uttered such lies" (Legat. 35); but he is writing in Greece, not in Gaul. Theophilus traces them to report (ad Autol. iii. 4). Tertullian again (ad Jud. 13), and Origen (c. Cels. vi. 27), ascribe them to Jews. Lecky thinks that these slanderous rumours "were greatly encouraged by the ecclesiastical rule" which veiled the Christian rites from the unbaptised (Hist. Europ. Morals, 441).

[2] Justin, Apol. ii. 12 ; cp. Tatian ad Græc. 25.

[3] Yet Lucian, in his De Morte Peregrini, ignores them; and cp. Euseb. iv. 7.

worst of these libels, a Christian passing along a street, in the early morning, to his Eucharist, would be pursued with cries which would mean the next thing to massacre: "Ah, there he goes to his blood-feast,—he and his have a poor little babe, all ready to be cut up and devoured;[1] they use their bread to sop up its blood, and *that's* their religion!" "So brutally did the imagination of the heathen mob play with the sacred feast on the Holy Flesh,"[2] even as, by another base blunder or another malicious invention, it perverted the meaning of that supper which Pliny's informants called "innocent," and which Tertullian described as true to its name of "Love," into an orgy of reckless vice.[3] After this, it was a light

---

[1] Cp. Tertull. Apol. 8.

[2] H. S. Holland, The Apostolic Fathers, p. 16. Tatian retorts the charge of cannibalism on pagan mythology (Ad Græcos, 25).

[3] Cp. Euseb. v. 1 (Letter of churches of Vienne and Lyons) and Athenagoras (Legat. 31 ff.). On the Agape, cp. above, p. 107.

thing to say that Christians worshipped the head of an ass,[1] or the cross,[2] which to Roman ears spelt gibbet,—that they were a "shirking, skulking race" that dared not meet by daylight,[3] or traitors to Rome because they would not swear by the "genius" or guardian spirit of the emperor.[4] Nor were those more atrocious misconstructions current only among the vulgar; educated men, who afterwards became Christians, had once believed them. A tutor of Marcus Aurelius countenanced the slander about the Agape;[5] and cultured agnostics, who

---

[1] The Alexamenos "graffito" represented a figure with an ass's head tied to a cross. Tertullian (Apol. 16) mentions a similar caricature, and traces this libel to a fiction in Tac. Hist. v. 3, about the Jews in the wilderness.

[2] Tert. *l.c.* Cp. Pusey's note.

[3] Minucius Felix, Octavius, 8.

[4] For Tertullian's reply to the charge of disloyalty, cp. Apol. 30 ff.

[5] Fronto; Octav. 31. It is observed that he had no evidence to cite, but simply "convicium, ut orator, adspersit." Yet he was an amiable man.

treated providential government as unthinkable, and professed to find no other first cause than fate or chance, were all the more intolerant of men and women stupid enough to believe in a God who took real account of human action, and would bring every thought into judgment.[1] "They can talk insufferable nonsense in that strain, and yet they are too scrupulous to join in the venerable ceremonies coeval with Rome's greatness!" From such persons, then,

[1] The pagan (Oct. 10) is made to say that the Christians imagine their God as minutely inspecting characters, acts, words, even secret thoughts, as "molestum, inquietum, *impudenter curiosum*"—a God, in short, who would not leave men alone. Cp. Tertull. Apol. 45, "ab incontemptibili Dispectore;" and De Testim. Animæ, 2, that some who do not deny that God exists, by no means regard Him as "dispectorem et arbitrum et judicem;" and Origen on "taking care not to say anything which they would not like to think of as reported to God" (c. Cels. iv. 26). Minucius probably had in mind the protest of Cicero's Epicurean (de Nat. Deor. i. 20) against the notion of "a *curiosus deus*, who thinks that everything is within his province." Of course the Christian idea of "an observant God" is bound up with belief in Him as a Father.

Christians had as little forbearance to expect as from the peasant who bowed down to some ugly rustic image, — and specially because they would not be content to rank their God with the "gods many," but insisted that if He were taken at all, He must needs be taken as all in all.[1] We can, then, easily understand that, if easy-going respectable pagans could say in a reflective, candid, and half-regretful tone, "So-and-so is a good fellow, *but* he is a Christian,"[2]—if abhorrence of Christianity could crush out natural affection, and make "fathers and brothers" fulfil Our Lord's prediction, as we are told was often the case[3]— the populace, especially when stirred up by fanatical priests, by diviners whom Christians were known to scorn as cheats, or by some of the miscellaneous dependents on the temple-

---

[1] Cp. Bp. Westcott, Epistles of St. John, p. 246 ff.
[2] Tertull. Apol. 3.
[3] Tertull. Scorp. 9, referring to Matt. x. 21.

worship, would be quite ready to plunder the houses of Christians, to put them (as at Lyons) under a sort of social ban, excluding them from baths or markets, to maltreat them if they appeared in the streets, and to invoke against them the action of public authority.[1]

(2.)

And so we come to the second part of our immediate subject. On what principle did

---

[1] See Euseb. v. 1. 5; cp. Melito, ib. iv. 26, on "pillaging by the rabble"; and Dionys. Alex., ib. vi. 41, on the popular persecution at Alexandria which preceded Decius' edict by a year, and made all streets, roads, or lanes, unsafe for Christians (cp. also Tertull. Apol. 35). Allard gives a vivid description of the miscellaneous crowds that thronged Lyons, the metropolis of three provinces, at the festival of "Rome and Augustus" on August 1, when, in 177, "une sorte de mot d'ordre, venu on ne sait d'où, tourna contre les chrétiens l'esprit mobile et déjà surexcité de la foule" (Hist. des Persèc. i. 392-395). Columns from the temple of Augustus adorn the venerable church of St. Martin d'Ainay (Athanacum, from "Athenæum") at Lyons, the crypt of which lies between dungeons associated by old traditions with this persecution.

the public authority of the Roman empire, speaking directly through the emperor, or through provincial magistrates as his representatives, rest its action when persecuting the Church? It was well understood that if any form of worship was officially pronounced "illicit" or unlawful, its presence on Roman ground was an offence, and the practice of its rites, or even the avowed intention of adhering to it, would be in official logic a capital crime.[1] Then came what we might call the minor premiss: "Christianity is thus unlicensed, is an illicit religion." It stood on a different platform from that which was occupied by Judaism, or by some weird

[1] "Toleration or indifference," such as was freely, even contemptuously, exhibited by the Roman state to opinions or beliefs as such, "found its own limits at once whenever the doctrine taught had a practical bearing on society," or "when a strange god and cultus could be brought into no affinity or corporate relation with Roman gods" (Döllinger, Gentile and Jew, ii. 162). This latter condition, it is true, existed in regard to the Jewish religion; but it had obtained special recognition as a purely national "cult."

un-Roman "cults" which had obtained the sanction of the government. The conclusion was inevitable, and was expressed in four Latin words, which became proverbial as a menace to Christians—*Non licet esse vos.*[1] "You, as Christians, have no legal existence; you stand condemned for your adherence to Christianity: it is not necessary to prove any other misdeeds against you." This was the maxim recognised by the imperial government in the second century; but when was it first put in force against the Christians? Accepting the First Epistle of St. Peter as a genuine apostolical work of the reign of Nero, we find that the Apostle either knew that it had been already acted on, or expected it to be acted on in the near future. For he bids the Christians of five districts of Asia Minor to take care that none of them incur punishment for what we should call felonies, "but if any one suffer as a

[1] Tertull. Apol. 4.

Christian, let him not be ashamed, but let him glorify God in this name," *i.e.* by suffering on account of it, simply because he is a Christian. This implies that Christianity was no longer safe as a supposed variety of Judaism,[1] that it had somehow already been made illicit; but this takes us back to the imputations made against it, which at this early period were chiefly political and social— " They have turned the world upside down : they act contrary to the decrees of Cæsar." From such complaints it was easy to pass to the charge of hostility to Roman society,[2] and thence to that of opposition to the worship of the Roman gods; and some at least of the worst libels already referred to had taken hold of the Roman popular mind.

---

[1] "Quasi sub umbraculo insignissimæ religionis, certe licitæ," Tertull. Apol. 21. Festus had evidently so regarded it, Acts xxv. 19, 25.

[2] That *odium humani generis* (Tac. Ann. xv. 44) refers to the *Roman* world—its laws, usages, and civilisation, cp. Prof. Ramsay, p. 236.

Here then were materials accumulated for an explosion. Rome was ready to say of Christianity what French unbelief has said of clericalism—"*There's* the enemy." "You treat us as foes, we will deal with you as with foes."[1] So it was that Nero, in the summer of 64, could provide for public amusement by setting a great number of Christians on fire to light up his Vatican gardens,[2] or exposing them to be mangled by dogs; this barbarous freak was part of his scheme for diverting to them the obloquy of the burning of Rome: but he branded them also as guilty of flagrant crimes, and educated Romans believed that, however innocent they might be of incendiarism, they still "deserved the extremity of punishment."[3] Whether

[1] "Religionem publico odio et hostili elogio obnoxiam" (Tertull. de Res. Carnis, 21). "Elogium" here = an indictment, as in Tert. ad Scap. 4.

[2] The scene of these horrors was on the left side of the present St. Peter's. There, too, afterwards, St. Peter was crucified, "between the two goals" of Nero's circus.

[3] "Novissima exempla meritos" (Tac. *l.c.*).

Nero did issue definite edicts proscribing Christians, as Sulpicius Severus in the fourth century asserts,[1] or whether provincial magistrates took their emperor's "humours for a warrant," a rapid inference would clench the matter: "Christians are believed to do this and that, to be thus and thus guilty, thus and thus dangerous to Rome and to public order; *therefore* Christianity, as a religion, ought not to exist." On either view, the Neronian cruelties were "the inauguration of a new policy," however little concern that "wild beast" may have had in the martyrdoms of St. Peter and St. Paul, the latter, of whom, at any rate, seems to have suffered after Nero had left Rome to the rule of "governors," as Clement calls them in the Epistle to the Church of Corinth. As far as records go, persecution seems to have slept

[1] Hist. Sacr. ii. 26. Sulpicius *may* have "modified or exaggerated" something in the lost books of Tacitus' Histories (cp. a review of Prof. Ramsay's book in the *Guardian*, May 17, 1893).

until Domitian,[1] who was intent on the propagation of Cæsar-worship, which he "looked upon as part of the national religion," put to death some Christians and sent others into exile: he assumed, no doubt, that as Christians, they *must* be disaffected. Among his victims was Flavius Clemens, already referred to, who was accused of "atheism" —the very charge so often brought against Christians,[2]—and also of the adoption of "Jewish" (meaning Christian) usages. His wife Domitilla was banished to an island, but probably returned after the tyrant's death.[3]

And now as to the famous instructions given by Trajan to Pliny the Younger, as

---

[1] Ramsay thinks that the first two Flavian emperors did persecute, although no record of such proceedings remains. St. Hilary brackets Vespasian with Nero and Decius (c. Aux. 2), but on what evidence?

[2] Cp. Lightfoot, St. Clement, i. 34.

[3] Her cemetery had been constructed on "a magnificent, almost royal" scale (De Rossi, Inscr. Chr. i. 2), before her exile.

governor of Bithynia. That emperor, for whom Gregory the Great is said to have expressed respect and admiration, did his best to minimise judicial proceedings against persons accused of being Christians: he forbade inquisitorial officiousness, and treated anonymous information as inadmissible.[1] Other emperors gave directions in a like sense—Hadrian being yet more severe than Trajan in his view of "calumniators;"[2] but the maxim that profession of Christianity, proved by evidence as to acts, and adhered to in the presence of a judge, was *per se* a capital offence, held its ground until the middle of the third century, and even then was but temporarily set aside.[3] If the offence in question were proved on reputable

[1] It was, he said tersely, "pessimi exempli," and did not suit the spirit of the age. On informers, cp. Melito in Euseb. iv. 26; and Gibbon, i. 225, 237.

[2] "If," he wrote, "the provincials can prove that Christians do anything against law," *e.g.* practise their worship.

[3] By the edicts of Gallienus, Euseb. vii. 13.

evidence, Trajan ruled that the law must take its course; it did so take its course under Trajan's successors, including Marcus Aurelius when consulted by the provincial government as to the Christian confessors of Lyons and Vienne.[1] It was vain for writers in defence of Christianity to complain of this ruling as unjust, and to claim that some other definite offence should be brought home to Christians before they were condemned:[2] the legal principle was intelligible, and it has been truly said[3] that it was often—though not always—the best of the emperors who, "as straightforward, patriotic, law-

---

[1] Marcus was personally prejudiced against the Christians, and they suffered much under his reign. Lightfoot says, that "with all his personal amiability, and all his philosophical training, he was a slave to the system under which he was educated," etc. (Hist. Essays, p. 36), and that "he was the most active promoter of Cæsar-worship" (SS. Ignat. and Polycarp. i. 450). But besides this, the self-sufficiency of his Stoicism would make Christianity, so far as he understood it, offensive to him.

[2] Justin, Apol. i. 7; Athen. 2; Tertull. Apol. 2.

[3] Lightfoot, SS. Ignat. and Polycarp, i. 17.

loving Roman statesmen, were invited by the responsibilities of their position to persecute," as a Decius struck, under a sense of public duty, at those whom a Commodus [1] had been persuaded to spare.

(3.)

To return to St. Peter's First Epistle. "Beloved," so runs his warning, "do not be amazed at the kindling of fire among you, which is coming upon you in order to try you." If, as the ancients thought, he was writing in Rome itself, the recollection of the incendiary troubles of Nero's eleventh year may have been in the Apostle's mind; but he is certainly using the familiar Biblical image of the application of fire to metal by way of test—the image which St. Paul had

---

[1] Refut. Hær. ix. 12. The Christian faith of a chamberlain of Commodus was intimated by a Christian freedman in an addition to his epitaph (De Rossi, Inscr. Chr. i. 9).

employed as to the awful future "day" which should "put every man's work to the proof." The Apostle of hope and courage, now more than ever a Cephas, a Petros, would fain infuse into his distant brethren somewhat of the "rock-like" firmness which can deliberately contemplate the *diræ facies* of the future, and refuse to be terrified or even discomposed. "It is only what you bargained for when you became disciples of the Crucified; it is thus that you are to have the honour of some share in 'Christ's sufferings,' to be 'overshadowed by the Spirit of glory and of God.'"[1] He would, for his own part, recall the Divine words spoken in the upper room on the eve of the Passion—"If the world hate you, you know that it hated Me" first, and "the servant is not greater than his lord."

---

[1] Perhaps it was 1 Pet. iv. 14 which suggested the proverbial saying embodied in Ignatius' letter to the Smyrnæans: "Near to sword, near to God."

Nero, we must always recollect, set on foot no general persecution. In fact, our best notions of what a general persecution was like must be taken from the time of Decius about two centuries later. Local persecutions there were many, and "fiery trials" they must have been to those who were exposed to them; a just emperor like Trajan, an impressionable emperor like Hadrian, might limit their scope; a lovable emperor like Antoninus might forbid Greek mobs to harass Christians, and might be personally irresponsible for such martyrdoms as that of Polycarp;[1] even a "hard-natured" emperor like Severus might so frame his penal decree as not to affect these who were already Christians,[2] or might retain some Christians about his person: but, the law being what it was, Christians held their immunity from day to day on a precarious

[1] Cp. Lightfoot, SS. Ignat. and Polyc. i. 443.
[2] What he thus forbade was "*fieri* Christianos."

tenure. And when an imperial edict did go forth, commanding all inhabitants of a district to come forward at a fixed time and sacrifice, or otherwise do public homage, to the gods, or else to abide the consequences of a refusal, we can imagine that the "burning" would be red-hot. A hundred years at least before Decius took seriously in hand the work of stamping out a religion which in his eyes was not only illicit, but prejudicial to the Empire in its political unity, and to the ideas and traditions which had made Rome great, Hermas had pictured the approach of a coming tribulation under the image of "a monster like a whale, coming on with a rush that might have destroyed a city;" and one of the four colours discernible on its head was to indicate the effect of the trial on those true Christians whom it would exhibit as pure "gold."[1] Yet all Christians, in prospect of such a "day of the Lord,"

---

[1] Vis. iv. 1.

would be more or less harassed by anxiety as to their own strength—would, according to Christ's prediction about His own Apostles in general, be shaken as wheat in a sieve.[1] And the sifting would be indeed a "great shaking" when the Christian had perforce to stand in his turn before the tribunal, and was commanded to recognise the gods of the Empire by some public act of worship. The genuine records of martyrdom (unfortunately there are not a few that are spurious) show that the answer, in many cases, was concisely resolute: "I do not" (that is, "I will not) sacrifice." But then would come remonstrances, kindly meant, though in effect so many temptations. We must not imagine that proconsuls or judges were always sanguinary or inhuman. Often enough they would be men of the class of

---

[1] Newman, Serm. ii. 45. Dion. Alex. says that when the edict of Decius reached Alexandria, *all cowered down* (Euseb. vi. 41). Cp. Tert. de Fugâ, 1, " in attonito."

Festus, humane and fair-minded from their own point of view.[1] They would do their best to save the accused, as they would regard it, from his own fanatical folly.[2] "Consider what you say; take time for second thoughts; don't throw away fair prospects, and plunge your friends into grief, for a mere superstitious fancy. You are young, and have life before you;" or,

---

[1] Tertullian mentions some who, though not humane, dismissed charges against Christians: one, for instance, said that to proceed against the accused would provoke a tumult; another expressed annoyance at having "lighted on such a case;" a third, "acting according to orders," tore up an indictment not authenticated by a name (ad Scap. 4). So a magistrate at Alexandria actually dismissed from his tribunal a Christian lad of fifteen, in sheer admiration of his courage (Euseb. vi. 41).

[2] *E.g.* in "Acts" of Scillitan martyrs: "You can obtain pardon from our lords the emperors, if," etc. So the proconsul to St. Polycarp: "Think of your age," etc.; and to St. Cyprian: "Consule tibi," etc. So in the story of the boy martyr Cyril: "I will forgive you," says the judge, "if you will but think of your own interests." So Tertullian quotes words used by "præsides:" "Save your life—don't throw away your life" (Scorp. 11).

it might be, "You are old, and cannot expect to live long; why anticipate death, when you might save at least some remnants of life, and pass away tranquilly, instead of perishing in such anguish as you will force me to inflict if you persist in senseless contumacy?" Probably there might follow the suggestion that what was required was, after all, a slight formal act; a single gesture would suffice for throwing a few grains of incense on that little altar close at hand: "Do this, and you satisfy the law; no inquiry is made into your opinions; we do not exact any verbal renunciation of Christ, although this, too, has in some cases been demanded;[1] but we will not press it upon *you*." This kind of language would be often more dangerous than any violent attack on Christianity, such as a hot-tempered judge might make by way of venting his scornful

---

[1] As when Polycarp was bidden to "revile Christ," and made his immortal reply. And cp. Pliny's letter.

disgust, or his zeal for the official worship or for the authority of Cæsar. And then would be seen the enervating effect of prolonged quiet and comfort on a Christian's moral tone. Those who had settled on their lees, and, as we have already noticed, had contracted pagan habits and worldly laxity from intimacies not formed "in the Lord,"[1] who had been "insatiably bent on enlarging their possessions,"[2] who had adopted a heathenish extravagance in "outward self-adornment,"[3] who had given their daughters to heathen husbands, who had let their tongues loose in outbreaks of bitterness, who had pushed quarrels to extremity,—who had, in short, become manifoldly secularised,—

[1] So Hermas speaks of some who lived much with pagans, and acquired a liking for their ways, although they retained their faith, and in many cases repented (Simil. viii. 9).

[2] Cp. Cypr. de Lapsis, 6, 7.

[3] Clement of Alexandria and Tertullian have much to say about the love of dress as a snare to Christian ladies.

were but too likely "to betray their faith at the first menace of the enemy." To this class would also belong Christians who had held civil office without taking care to preserve their spiritual loyalty; and we read that in an Alexandrian persecution the heathen friends of some weak Christians would importune them to commit themselves at once by sacrificing, while their pallor and trembling excited the mockery of heathen bystanders — in contrast to the dreadful readiness with which others, who had never really had a "trace" of living faith, "ran up to the tribunals" and exclaimed, "I never was a Christian!" or even when the magistrate was leaving his tribunal in the evening, besought him not to defer until the morrow his acceptance of their conformity to the edict.[1] Others, perhaps some who, as Origen says, "had often *shone* in the Churches,"[2]

---

[1] Dionys. Alex. in Euseb. vi. 41 ; Cypr. de Lapsis, 8.
[2] Exhort. ad Mart. 18.

would at first witness a good confession, would say, not once nor twice, "I am a Christian;" then would follow other attempts to break down their constancy — severe scourging, imprisonment in the horrible dens or pits of a "carcer,"[1] with feet made fast in the stocks,[2] and perhaps for weeks of slow starvation amid a fetid atmosphere,[3] or if this failed, then torture in that variety of forms which Christian governments, to their shame, took over from pagan imperialism—

[1] The inner prison was called "lignum;" a trap-door in it opened into the dungeon or "robur," like the "Tullianum" in the Mamertine (Sallust. Cat. 55).

[2] Origen's feet were "stretched to the fourth hole" (Euseb. vi. 39; cp. v. 1. 22).

[3] Cp. Cypr. Ep. 22, 237. 2. Perpetua says, "We were put into the prison, and I shuddered, because I had never experienced such darkness" (Ruinart, Act. Sinc. p. 138). Cp. Tertull. de Res. Carnis, 8, ad Martyres, 2, on the darkness, filth, chains, vile food, foul air, which made life in a prison so wretched. To these was often added the infliction of the stocks (cp. Acts xvi. 24), tortures, and even death by suffocation (Euseb. v. 1. 22). Penal servitude in the mines is referred to in Cypr. Ep. 76. 1; 77. 3 (cp. Euseb. Mart. Pal. 5).

so that Cyprian could with his noble equity represent some who had given way under "scourge, or club, or rack, or flame," as having good right to plead for the Church's forgiveness on the ground of "weakness of flesh" amid intense and protracted agony.[1] The Church might restore such persons to communion after a certain amount of penance; but she had simply to praise God for the persistent heroism of martyrs,[2] which to the heathen spectators appeared nothing better than a dogged, brutal, irrational "obstinacy," a "reckless and desperate"

---

[1] Cypr. de Lapsis, 13; cp. ad Demetr. 12: "Longa tormenta . . . ingeniosa crudelitas;" and Tertull. de Res. Carnis, 8, "omni tormentorum machinatione."

[2] This is beautifully brought out by Milman in his "Martyr of Antioch"—

"Sing to the Lord! it is not shed in vain,
　The blood of martyrs; from its freshening rain
　High springs the Church, like some fount-shadowing palm."

Even in Tertullian's time hymns were written and sung in honour of martyrdom (Scorp. 7).

throwing away of life;[1] as even the good Marcus Aurelius had called it a "challenge"[2] ostentatiously addressed to authority, which that authority was therefore bound to take up. "If you want to die," said a proconsul, "can't you find halters and precipices enough?"[3] But there were those to whom, as Tertullian says, this same supposed "obstinacy" was salutary "teaching." We have evidence enough that the sight of a martyrdom, the moral majesty of endurance unto death for a deep-seated conviction, was repeatedly the very impulse required to make men decide for Christ as the rightful Sovereign of souls. The pruning of the vine, said one who himself became a martyr, did but produce new shoots;[4] or, in the

---

[1] Tertull. Apol. 27, 50. So Pliny had "no doubt that *pervicacia* and *inflexibilis obstinatio* ought to be punished, whatever the accused might confess."

[2] This seems to be the sense of his word παράταξις.

[3] Tertull. ad Scap. 5.

[4] Justin, Dial. 110.

terse phrase which caught the Christian ear, and was circulated as a proverb, the blood of Christians proved to be seed if, where it was spilt, there sprung up a new crop of conversions.[1] We cannot wonder that martyrdom, on the part of a catechumen, was believed to supply the place of baptism, and was called "a baptism of blood."[2] That, *sicut humanum est*, there were spots amid this splendour; that sometimes one could wish that "there had been more self-restraint, more quietness and calm in the very eye of the storm, amid the provoking of all men;"[3] that admiration for these "mighty men" of the sacred Kingdom often became unbalanced,

---

[1] Tertull. Apol. 50; cp. Aug. in Ps. 39. 1. In his Ad Scap. 5 Tertullian varies the image; the Church is never so truly being "built up as when it seems to be cut down; for every one" (he means, many persons) "beholding such firm endurance (of martyrs) is impelled to ask what causes it; and when he has ascertained the truth (on that point), et ipse statim sequitur" (cp. Origen, c. Cels. iv. 32).

[2] Tert. de Bapt. 16; Cyprian, Ep. 73. 21, etc.

[3] Church, Cath. and Univ. Serm. p. 279.

and gradually prepared an entrance for superstition;[1]—that their numbers have been exaggerated, and that invention was set to work upon their story in default of evidence,[2]—does not abate the justice of a great English Christian's observation, that we "do not half enough consider the excellence of this martyr spirit."[3] In thinking of them as a

---

[1] Even confessors, as at Carthage, were sometimes betrayed by the homage they received into presumptuous abuse of their privilege of asking the Church to shorten the penance-time of the lapsed (cp. Cypr. Ep. 23; 27. 2). Visits to the tombs of martyrs suggested and extended the practice of invoking their intercession with God. (Cp. Dict. Chr. Ant. i. 857.)

[2] Allard contends that the theory which greatly diminished the number of martyrs has been corrected by archæological discoveries, which have shown that even in *passiones* which are on the whole untrustworthy some traces of fact are recoverable (Hist. des Perséc. i. p. 10 ff.). Origen's words (c. Cels. iii. 8)—which Gibbon misquotes—mean only (as the context shows) that martyrs were "few" in comparison with the whole Christian body (cp. ib. i. 26; ii. 17).

[3] So wrote Dr. Arnold in July, 1840, after looking at that wonderful "series of pictures" which inflicts on the modern visitor, as he walks round the circular church of San Stefano on the Cælian, so vivid and appalling a

Question of Flight from Persecution.

"white-robed host," whose faith, then taking its completest form, did most conspicuously overcome the world, we must not forget the multitude of sufferers for Christ whose confessorship was not consummated by martyrdom. Persecutions, in the proper sense, brought to the front several questions of casuistry: was it in any case permissible to flee from one city to another? Montanists said, "No, never;"[1] but the Church, on the whole, said "Yes"—at least in some cases; for there would be circumstances in which even a bishop, for instance, would do best by living for his flock, though under other conditions the pastors would feel called upon to set their people an example of constancy.[2]

---

sense of what Christians had often to endure, if they resolutely followed in the track of Stephen and of Antipas (cp. Stanley's Life of Arnold, ii. 404).

[1] Tertullian had once thought flight lawful (ad Ux. i. 3); but in his De Fugâ he condemns it, treating Matt. x. 23 as a temporary direction. His argument (ib. 4) would prove it wrong to avoid *any* calamity.

[2] St. Polycarp, "persuaded by his friends," retired

There would be not a few lay Christians who, if flight were difficult, would resort to evasive methods of escaping the full force of the trial which, to their physical temperament, appeared overwhelming: they would secretly give fees to officers of justice, or procure, doubtless also by bribes, official certificates that they had satisfied the law.[1]

first to one farm, then to another, where he was arrested (Euseb. iv. 15). Dionysius of Alexandria believed himself to have been divinely warned to flee, but after he had fled and been arrested, he tried to resist a party of friends, bent on rescuing him (ib. vi. 40). Cyprian's retirement was disapproved of by the Roman clergy (Cypr. Ep. 8); he explained that he had wished to prevent an increase of pagan agitation (Ep. 20. 1; cp. Ep. 43. 4). One hardly sees on what evidence it can be said that "the earlier tone of the Church" approved of "voluntarily offering one's self for martyrdom" (Ramsay, Ch. in R. Empire, p. 433). Lucian (whose bias is obvious) says that "the majority voluntarily give themselves up" (de Mort. Per. 13); but the Smyrnæan circular was understood by Eusebius to blame such conduct as "not in accordance with piety."

[1] Hence they were called "libellatici" (cp. Cyprian, Ep. 55. 14). He speaks of them severely, *e.g.* "qui ne fandis libellis . . . conscientiam polluissent" (Ep. 20. 2; cp. De Laps. 27). But he distinctly treats them as less guilty than those who had actually taken part, under

To do so was constructively to lie, and also professedly to range themselves among deniers of Christ; but they argued that it was, at any rate, better than the apostasy into which, otherwise, they assumed that they would be betrayed by terror or positive suffering. They afterwards declared their sorrow for their subterfuge; and penances were imposed on them, as also, in graduated measure, on those who had actually lapsed after mere menaces, or after this or that amount of imprisonment or of torture.

pressure, in idolatrous acts. One form of a *libellus* would be somewhat like this: "To those presiding over the sacrifices in such a place; I, A. B., have, in your presence, poured libations, etc., and I request you to give me a certificate to that effect." This, when signed by the official addressed, would be producible in bar of further proceedings (cp. the *Guardian* of March 21, 1894). Another would be simply a statement received from a magistrate, who had been privately informed of the applicant's Christianity. To procure immunity from penalties by bribing a magistrate was common enough under the empire (Acts xxiv. 26); and Tertullian, as a Montanist, broadly accuses Churchmen of resorting to his expedient, and warns them that they cannot thus disarm *popular* hostility (De Fugâ, 12 ff.).

This must suffice as to the official persecutions. Their number and their intensity have been overstated—they were the exception, not the rule; but, while they lasted, they were tests which "pierced to the dividing of soul and spirit." At the same time, they were overruled for good, both in the present and in the future. They broke in with an opportune sternness on that "security," in the Shakespearian sense of the term, into which Christians so easily drifted under such a reign, for instance, as that of Alexander Severus—the gentle eclectic who scrupled not to express, both privately and publicly, his respect for their worship and their ways.[1] When the Church "had rest," her average members would be too apt to forget the precept about loins girded and lamps burning; and then it was well that a thundering shock

---

[1] Cp. Lampridius, Vit. Alex. Sev. 29, 49. "His household consisted of many believers" (Euseb. vi. 28). Dionysius says the like of Valerian's at the outset of his reign (ib. vii. 10). On Diocletian's, cp. ib. viii. 1.

should "warn" those slumberers "ere it grew too late." And the many instances of an absolute self-devotion which these fiery trials called forth were signs which added force to the moral argument for the religion of those martyrs who testified, at the cost of life, to Him in whom was supremely realised the idea of a witness to the truth, who

> "in the garden secretly,
> And on the Cross on high,
> Could teach His brethren, and inspire
> To suffer and to die." [1]

---

[1] The same thought appears in Christina Rossetti's wonderful "Martyrs' Song:"

> " Death is short and life is long :
> Satan is strong, but Christ more strong.
> At His word, who hath brought us hither,
> The Red Sea must part hither and thither.
> . . . Yet one pang searching and sore,
> And then Heaven for evermore. . . .
> Yet one effort by Christ His grace,
> Then Christ for ever, face to face!"

ADDRESS V.

Archbishop Trench, in his excellent little book on "The Study of Words," refers to a class of instances in which an alteration for the worse in the sense of a term is a "testimony" to human "deterioration" or human "infirmity." Thus "apology," which by rights is simply a defence of one's own case, reminds us in its present use that cases are often weak, and that confessions of error are often due.[1] The true force of the original word, in this latter instance, was brought home with unique power to English minds by the title of Cardinal Newman's

---

[1] George III.'s naïve question as to Bishop Watson's "Apology for the Bible" is well known. The difference between *retractatio* and "retractation" is another case in point. Cp. Trench, p. 34.

most characteristic work. And so we may say that the Church of Christ has from the first had to make her *Apologia pro vitâ suâ.* St. Paul[1] uses the original term twice in one context, "In my defence and maintenance of the Gospel," and, still more pointedly, "I am stationed for the defence of the Gospel,"—it is my business to uphold its truth against all gainsayers; and St. Peter,[2] writing, as we have seen, in expectation of a persecution, exhorts Christians to "sanctify Christ in their hearts as Lord," to enthrone Him as a Divine Sovereign in the centre of their moral being,—and then significantly adds that part of this duty to Him consists in a "constant readiness to give an answer"— literally, "to make defence, *apologia*, to every man who asks of them a reason concerning the hope that is in them." As if to say, "You must not allow the cause of the faith, the cause of Christ, to 'take any

---

[1] Phil. i. 7, 16.   [2] 1 Pet. iii. 15.

hurt or hindrance by reason of your negligence' to set forth and support its claims: they can be stated, and reasons given for acknowledging them; if you let this matter go by default, you fail in spiritual loyalty." In another passage, where the word is not used,[1] St. Paul indicates his own method of "commending" his advocacy to "the conscience;" it is an ingenuous exposition of Christian truth in its positive form. We may well observe the connection of this method with the "conscience" of the hearer or reader. St. Paul is, as it were, the Apostle of conscience; whether his theme is the nullity of idols, or the moral condition of those Gentiles who, "having no law, show the work of the law written in their hearts," it is alike natural to him to appeal to this interior moral faculty. These surely are fruitful hints for the discharge of "apologetic" duty; and they were by no means

[1] 2 Cor. iv. 2.

the only contribution which the "Teacher of the Gentiles" made to that object. He could on occasion say hard words about "philosophy," could contrast his own position as a preacher of Christ crucified with that of Greeks who sought after "wisdom"—that is, for a "satisfactory" theory, and could mark for avoidance the "knowledge falsely so called," in its attitude of "opposition" to the deposit of truth;[1] but he was clearly thinking of the pretensions of a self-satisfied and secular intellectualism, and took care to add that the Gospel of Christ contained a real "wisdom," long hidden, but now unveiled. He did not go to work to meet the philosophy of the day on lines of direct argument, although he would incidentally allude to lines of Greek poetry, or take a Greek inscription as his text for an address on the Divine character; but while deprecating a

---

[1] Col. ii. 8, "Through *his* philosophy and vain deceit" (R.V.); 1 Cor. i. 22, 23; 1 Tim. vi. 20.

reference to the "psychical" or non-spiritual mind on "the things of the Spirit of God," he assumes, as of course, that Christian doctrine is "capable of a reasonable explanation," that it harmonises with "facts and laws of man's intellectual and moral nature."[1] The Christian apologist, then, as a student of St. Paul, would appeal to reason as not merely intellectual, but also moral and spiritual, the reason of the whole man as "a rationally and morally self-conscious spiritual personality."[2]

(1.)

This may seem a long preface to such a cursory survey of the primitive "Apologetic" as is alone possible in this address. But the relation between it and the unsystematic language of St. Paul is real and important;

---

[1] Duke of Argyll, Philosophy of Belief, p. 441. He is referring particularly to 1 Cor. viii. 1 ff.

[2] Moberly, Reason and Religion, p. 37.

and in its more persuasive forms it seems to have looked back instinctively to him who "became all things to all men" as to a model of self-adapting sympathy. Justin, known specifically as "the Martyr,"[1] had

---

[1] Justin was junior to Quadratus, from whose Apology, addressed to Hadrian, Eusebius (iv. 3) gives a remarkable extract, to the effect that some who had been the subjects of Our Lord's gracious miracles had survived to his own time. Eusebius dates the Apology of Aristides in the reign of Hadrian, and calls him an Athenian philosopher. On the Greek discourse, imbedded in the romance of Barlaam and Josaphat, and looking like a short form of the Syriac "Apology" recently discovered at Mount Sinai, see Prof. Robinson in "The Apology of Aristides," No. 1 of "Texts and Studies." He considers it to be (except in a few modifications, required for its insertion in the romance) more trustworthy than the Syriac. Yet the writer can hardly, one would think, be an educated Greek Christian of the first half of the second century. He attributes the theories which place deity in the sky or earth, water, fire, or air, to "Chaldæan philosophers," and the Greek wise men are for him simply the authors of an immoral mythology. The most interesting parts of the speech are the assertion of the Incarnation; Jesus Christ is identified with "the Son of God, who came down from heaven and was born of a holy virgin, assumed flesh, and appeared unto men, voluntarily endured death, rose

spent years in the search for truth, had tried one school after another, and at last had been led by the talk of an old man on the seashore of Palestine to find what he longed for in Christianity :—

> "The word which I had longed to hear
> Was come at last, the lifeful word." [1]

He caught at the idea of a great Light that through all ages, in various degrees, had been enlightening those who would receive it, not only within, but also in various

again, ascended into heaven;" and the summary of Christian morals, including an allusion to martyrdom.

[1] Trench's Poems, i. 19: "The Story of Justin Martyr." The confusion of tongues among the various philosophical schools was naturally a common Christian "topic." Tertullian insists on it: "Even when they agree you can find out that they differ" (De Anima, 2). And in the Pseudo-Clementine Recognitions, i. 3, Clement is described as stating his experience—nothing but assertion and counter-assertion, contests about words, display of dialectic ability. Hermias (of whose age nothing is known) wrote a satirical pamphlet called "Mockery" (lit. "a pulling to pieces") "of the Philosophers" outside the Christian pale. "One opinion drives out another. The upshot is that inquiry goes on *ad infinitum* with no tenable result." This is his line.

degrees outside the bounds of a special "covenant:" the Divine Word had been depositing in receptive minds a "word containing germs" or "seeds" of truth,[1] by way of preparation for His complete manifestation as incarnate in Christ. This implied that He had been all along and everywhere,—more fully, no doubt, among the chosen Hebrew race, but partially among all who were sons of peace,—the "invisible Guide" of man, the Inspirer of all high and noble thoughts which—

> "Through many a dreary age
> Upbore whate'er of good and wise
> Yet lived in bard or sage:"[2]

so that it was not a paradox to affirm a true kinship between such thoughts and the Christian revelation, nor any disparagement of faith to say that the reasonable faculties

---

[1] Apol. ii. 8. 10, 13.
[2] Maurice, Kingdom of Christ, i. 36; Christian Year, Fourth Sunday after Trinity. Cp. a noble context in Gladstone's Gleanings, vii. 33 ff.

of human nature were a divinely provided means of attaining to it.[1] Justin is not to be ranked among trained theologians, nor is his reasoning always exact:[2] but this conception of a universal Light, dimmer here and more vivid there, yet still a true Light for all, was beautiful and inspiring, and was destined to have wide issues; and the longer and more treatise-like of his two Apologies dwells earnestly on the ethical power of the

[1] The language is striking; through these powers which God has bestowed, He "both persuades and leads us to faith" (Apol. i. 10). Although it is strange that in an address to an emperor and to princes Justin should dwell so much on the argument from Hebrew prophecy, he goes straight to the mark when he repels the charges of atheism and political disaffection. The conclusion of his plea, as contained in the first of his two "Apologies," has all the dignity of what the Apostle calls "assured conviction": "We forewarn you that if you persist in your injustice, you will not escape the future judgment of God: and we will say boldly, The will of God be done." This is a breath of what Macaulay calls the spirit that "revived in Athanasius and Ambrose" (Misc. Writings, p. 352).

[2] But "in considering his theology it will be well to remember that we only possess his exoteric utterances" (Dict. Chr. Biogr. iii. 571).

Gospel, the innocence and strictness of Christian life, and the pure dignity of Christian worship.

The anonymous Epistle to Diognetus—apologetic in the sense of being addressed to a serious inquirer—was formerly ascribed to Justin; but although its writer *may* belong to the same period,[1] he takes a much less sympathetic view of Greek philosophy, and refers to Judaism simply as superstitious. In his account of the Christians as a body he agrees on the whole with other apologists.

---

[1] The date has been variously assigned to the close of the reign of Trajan, to Justin's own time, to the close of the century, or even later. In c. 3 the Jewish sacrificial system is referred to as if still in force. From c. 6, 7 we infer that persecution of Christians was active. The author may be identified with the writer of a short Discourse to Greeks, wrongly included among the works of Justin, and attributed, in a Syriac form, to Ambrosius, a "leading Greek" convert; Cureton, Spic. Syr. p. xi. He identifies this Ambrosius with Origen's friend of that name; but a writer in Dict. Chr. Biogr. iii. 163 ff. places him in the reign of M. Aurelius. Some of his language might suggest that he was adopting, for literary purposes, the tone of a sub-apostolic writer.

He is anxious to show that they conform to existing customs in matters indifferent, and "affect no singularity of behaviour; they obey the prescribed laws, but exceed them in their own lives; they dwell in the world, but are not of it; they are in the flesh, but do not live after the flesh." Here lies the contrast between them and all non-Christians. The gem of this little book is its account of the Incarnation and the Atonement. God, in His own time, and not sooner,[1] when human sin had come to its full development, exhibited His transcendent philanthropy by sending to us no ministering subordinate or angel, "but the very Maker of the universe, His own Son, in sweet exchange of the Holy One for the lawless, of the Innocent for the wicked;" for nought

---

[1] The natural pagan question, "Why was the coming of a Saviour of men, such as you say Christ is, so long delayed?" is also met by Origen, c. Cels. vi. 78; cp. Arnobius, ii. 75. St. Paul had already hinted the answer, Gal. iv. 4 (cp. Acts xvii. 30).

"but His righteousness could have covered our sins," and no otherwise "could we, the ungodly, have been justified than by the righteousness of One." This context is illustrated by the remark, that God is not to be imitated by domineering self-assertion, but by sympathetic and beneficent self-sacrifice. The last two chapters have been assigned to a different writer; but they may be simply a peroration in homiletic form.

(2.)

There is a yet more striking difference between the apologetic tone of Justin and that of a junior contemporary. His Assyrian pupil, Tatian, who compiled the first "Harmony of the Gospels," and ultimately became, as Irenæus puts it, "a combination of all the heretics," appears to take a grim delight in affronting the prepossessions of Greek students, and setting down philosophers as bad in the lump.¹ But we are again in Justin's atmosphere when Athenagoras, in the reign of Marcus Aurelius, appears as "ambassador for the Christians," and meets the charge of "atheism" on philosophical grounds, attacking the popular polytheism, and not omitting to notice the plea made by educated pagans that worship addressed to images (known to be mere images) was in fact received by the unseen deities themselves.² Theophilus, bishop of Antioch, who wrote soon after Athenagoras, in the early part of the reign of Commodus, had him-

---

[1] He had expected too much from Greek philosophy, and disappointment produced a vehement recoil. He had little power of mental balance.

[2] The apologetic "oration" existing in a Syriac form, and ascribed to Melito, contains no part of that "memorial" or petition to "Antoninus" (Marcus) from which Eusebius quotes a few sentences appealing to that emperor on behalf of Christians (iv. 26). Cp. the fragment in Pitra, Spic. Solesm. ii. p. xxxviii. ff.; Cureton, Spic. Syr. p. 41 ff. It has been thought to be an earlier work of Melito's; but cp. Salmon in Dict. Chr. Biogr. iii. 895.

self been converted by that evidence from prophecy which was made more of by these ancient advocates of the Faith than the evidence from miracles.[1] Theophilus has a majestic idea of God, as discernible by the spiritual being of man;[2] and while he relies on nature as witnessing to Him, insists on the moral conditions of truly seeing Him: "Trust yourself to the Physician,—to God who heals and gives life through His Word and His Wisdom,—and He will couch the eyes of your soul and heart."[3] This is in

---

[1] Theoph. ad Autol. i. 14.

[2] "If you say, 'Show me your God,' I would answer, 'Show me your man'" (*i.e.* your inward being), "and I will show you my God" (ad Autol. i. 2).

[3] Ad Autol. i. 7. Theophilus speaks of the Word as "immanent" in God until He was "begotten" as an agent in the creation of all things, and so became an "uttered" Word, or "Son" (ad Aut. ii. 10, 22). Newman observes that here "the philosophical words *endiathetic* and *prophoric*," which had been "implied as ideas" in other writings, "at length come to the surface;" and "further, Theophilus knows of no other *genesis* than the temporal" (Tracts Theol. and Eccl. p. 210). But he does not doubt that Theophilus, like other writers of his

Justin's own vein, and so is the subsequent remark that trust is a reasonable principle. Theophilus does not forget to pillory the foul figures of pagan mythology, or the inconsistent theology of poets and philosophers; and here he is more of a rigorist than some other apologists when he asks, "What good did Plato's system do him?" The most valuable passage in his work is a concise summary of Christian ethics as securing self-control in all forms, "the practice of righteousness, the extirpation of sin, the recognition of the only God."[1] "Truth governs, grace guards, peace overshadows them, the holy word guides, wisdom teaches, God reigns over them." Here, he would say,

class, believed the Word, while immanent, to be no mere attribute, but hypostatic (ib. 182, 198). It is well known that Theophilus introduced the theological use of the word "Trinity" (ad Autol. ii. 15).

[1] Ib. iii. 15, 23. He had already utilised Greek tragedians as witnesses for the truth of retributive judgment—*e.g.* in an Æschylean fragment—

"What ill thou dost, bethink thee, Some One sees."

is the intrinsic, inexhaustible attraction of Christianity for those who will seriously bring the facts to bear on those heathen calumnies with which "rumour has pre-occupied the minds of men," or on the easy-going popular assumption that its doctrines are incapable of proof, that it is, on the face of it, "silly" or absurd—for this the Christians of that early time had to bear;[1] and we are not better than our fathers.

(3.)

But what Justin planted was specially watered by Clement of Alexandria. He, too, had made his way out of paganism by the aid of various teachers, notably of one who, before presiding over the catechetical school, so-called, of Alexandria—an institution for

---

[1] The Christian doctrine of judgment, etc., was set down "vanitati et stupori, et, ut dicitur, *præsumptioni*," Tertull. de Test. Animæ, 4. "Præsumptio" = pre-assumption dispensing with reasoning.

preparatory Christian instruction on intellectual lines[1] in a city full of inquirers and students—had illustrated the practical aim of his religious thought by going forth as a missionary to the "Indians."[2] Clement, his successor, was eminently qualified for one side of apologetic work. He was signally affectionate and open-hearted, abounding in mental and moral sympathies; a man of very wide reading, which sometimes shows itself in what to moderns looks like pedantry, and in illustrative references so luxuriant and various that one often cannot see the cloth for the embroidery.[3] Newman has said, rather unkindly, of

[1] For an admirably vivid account of this "school," cp. Bigg, Bamp. Lect. p. 41.
[2] On Pantænus, cp. Euseb. iv. 10.
[3] Nothing comes amiss to him in this line; quotation follows quotation, one image hurries after another in a bewildering rush; matters of food, dress, customs, ceremonial, antiquities; cooks examining a sheep, farmers watering their fields, hunters tracking game with dogs, even a barring-out by schoolboys, find a place in his extraordinary picture-gallery.

Jeremy Taylor, that in his "literary resources" he is alike "inexhaustible" and "pointless:"[1] and a critic might say the like of Clement, who had accumulated much more learning than he could either digest or arrange. It is amusing, sometimes provoking, to see how his erudition runs away with him, how uncritical and unsystematic his mind is,[2] how characteristic the title of "Patchwork" as applied to his longest composition.[3] Yet is he, for all that, a very engaging and lovable writer; as a teacher he must have been charming to the pupils whom he was striving to draw onward and upward as "with cords of a man." For he had a contagious spiritual enthusiasm, a

---

[1] Lect. on Univ. Education, p. 221, ed. i.

[2] Cp. Bigg, Bamp. Lect. p. 46; and cp. Cruttwell, Lit. Hist. of Early Christianity, ii. 442.

[3] Clement says that the irregularity of form in these Miscellanies is intentional—in order to stimulate the reader's attention (Strom. vi. 2). In a later passage he gives another reason, connected with the *disciplina arcani*, vii. 110. He has a deep respect for Church tradition.

glowing love for souls, and a profound devotion to the "true," "loving," and "good Father," whose love for men is like that of a mother-bird for her young,[1] and to Christ as the gracious "Tutor" or Guide of conduct,[2] the "supremely lovable Saviour," the "God who suffered and is adored," who "does indeed desire to bestow the gift of immortality."[3] One might imagine him as continually looking upward, with "Lead, kindly Light," upon his lips. But, living

---

[1] Cohort. 91. Cp. ib. 94, "This tender Father of ours, the Father indeed."

[2] He expressly says that the idea of a "pedagogue" is ethical, not intellectual—not of a teacher, but of a trainer, (Pæd. i. 1). The pedagogue in a Greek family had to look after the boy's conduct and behaviour; he was precisely *not* a "schoolmaster," but a "tutor" in the older and more accurate sense of the word. Clement's three treatises represented the natural sequence of exhortation, discipline, and instruction.

[3] Strom. ii. 20; Cohort. 106, 120. Very characteristic are his words in Strom. iv. 113, "Christ, that is, the presence of the Lord who loves us, and that *loving teaching* and mode of life of ours which is according to Christ." He is very fond of the words "philanthropy, philanthropic."

and lecturing and writing in a great meeting-place of theories, which naturally encouraged an excessive eclecticism, and eagerly striving, in a somewhat optimistic spirit, to utilise the current philosophies as capable of aiding the intelligent seeker after God,[1] Clement became too vague as a Christian teacher; theology in his hands took a one-sided

[1] Many Christians in his time were, as he puts it, "frightened by Greek philosophy as children by a mask" (Strom. vi. 80, cp. ib. 89). They thought it would "lead them away" from faith. He tells them that their faith must be so weak as to be not worth having, and reminds them of the duty of "testing and distinguishing." In his view nearly all the Greek schools, however defective (and he distinctly says that, even at their best, they fell short of Christianity, ib. i. 98), had a hold on some valuable germs of truth; and these could be combined and developed by the full truth now revealed (ib. i. 57). A narrow-minded Christian might look askance at secular knowledge, and ask, *e.g.*, "What's the good of logic?" (ib. vi. 93); but a thoughtful Christian would use learning of all kinds, and claim all true and noble sayings for the service of Christ (ib. i. 43. 44). Cp. also Strom. i. 28, 99; vi. 62, 67, 153; on philosophy in its best form as a "preparatory education." But he excludes the philosophies which deny providence or materialise God (Strom. i. 50).

development; Christianity was viewed too much from an academical standpoint, as a religion of illuminative rather than of redemptive efficacy; and while the need of a moral healer was recognised, salvation appeared rather as delivering from the tyranny of evil habit than as extending to the removal of guilt.[1] Thus the characteristics of the Pauline Gospel were not a little obscured,[2] and "grace" might seem to melt into a refined and elevated "nature." Moreover, Clement "Platonises" so much, that the idea or principle underlying an event or an institution sometimes appears to be for him alone of value, although a second reading may modify the impression:[3] it takes some

---

[1] See Pædag. i. 83, 100.

[2] Dr. Bigg even says that "Clement only half understood St. Paul" (Bamp. Lect. p. 83).

[3] His idealising vein shows itself in his attempt to Christianise the impassive "wise man" of the Stores: he so far forgets the Gospel narrative as to assert that Christ was inaccessible to feeling (Strom. vi. 71). See a sample of extravagant mysticism in Strom. vi. 133 ff.

time for the reader to get a grip of the actual thing in question; what it adumbrates, illustrates, symbolises, when looked at thus or thus, obscures what it *is*.[1] All this dreaminess, as one is apt to call it, is in singular contrast with his readiness as a

---

[1] His language about John vi. 53 is a case in point. He speaks of Christ's "flesh" as "allegorically" representing the Holy Spirit, of His blood as "darkly hinting" at the Word, or faith (using the verbs ἀλληγορεῖν and αἰνίττεσθαι), and again he says that the flesh and blood mean full spiritual "comprehension" (cp. Pæd. i. 43, 38; Strom. vi. 66). To infer that he did not admit a more primary sense of these sacred terms would be to prove too much, for he deals in a similar way with the sacrifice of Isaac, the feeding of the five thousand, and the anointing of Our Lord's feet (Strom. ii. 20; vi. 94; Pæd. ii. 61), here following St. Paul's use of the story of Hagar. The fact is, Clement recognises facts of this kind, but prefers to dwell on the ideas which they suggest to him: he catches eagerly at spiritual applications, one after another, as they occur; but the things or events themselves are neither ignored nor intentionally disparaged. He regards the Eucharist as "hallowed food" (Strom. iv. 161), and in one passage extols it as χάρις ἐπαινουμένη, interpreting the "blood" to mean the "active principle" of the Word, *i.e.* as incarnate (Pæd. ii. 19, 20). His language shows that he did not identify the Agape as such with the Holy Communion.

moralist to descend into the homeliest particulars of behaviour;[1] and he is perspicuous enough when exposing the fallacy of the pagan-conservative plea for "ancestral custom," or associating Christian faith with man's true dignity, or arguing from its moral effects on human life.[2] And on the whole, after all deductions which can fairly be made, Clement exemplifies well the religious teacher's duty of really entering into the mind of the learner, of attracting whatever in him is worthiest,[3] of blessing and not banning the secular or literary side of his studies; and he did excellent service to the

[1] *E.g.* A Christian should be composed and tranquil; therefore, keep your eyes steady and your hands quiet at table, etc. (Pædag. ii. 61). A wife who makes her husband's meals comfortable "will be approved by the Pædagogus" (ib. iii. 49). Cp. Cohort. 100.

[2] Cohort. 89, 93, 107.

[3] In Strom. ii. 26, Clement uses the illustration of the magnet to set forth the attraction which religious truth has for responsive souls. Newman says that he had a "dread of loading or formalising the mind" (The Arians, p. 50).

whole Christian cause by vindicating the naturalness and reasonableness of faith as a principle,[1] by emphasising the fact of moral freedom and personal responsibility,[2] and by alluring fair and serious minds to "see Jesus," to find in Him the satisfaction of deepest needs, and the practical solution of the question of life.[3] One might summarise the Apologetic of Clement in a single line of Keble's—

"By its own light the truth is seen."

---

[1] Cp. Strom. ii. 8, 9, 14, 16, 30 ff.; vii. 55, 57. Faith is vindicated against Gentile or Gnostic disparagement. It is not a conjecture, nor a result of natural temperament, nor a product of fear, but an intuitive movement of the soul towards primary truths, in accordance with laws which govern all thought; an act implying free choice, leading to repentance and hope, and consummated in knowledge and in love. So in Cohort. 95, faith is called an "innate and competent witness." Yet, as a rule, his estimate of faith is far too low (Cruttwell, Lit. Hist. Early Christ. ii. 456), in that he regards it as superseded by "knowledge" in the case of the more intellectual Christians, who as such are elevated into a kind of aristocracy.

[2] Strom. i. 83, 89.

[3] Christian Year, St. Bartholomew. In Cohort. 68, Clement anticipates "Sun of my soul."

(4.)

As Justin leads to Clement, so Clement leads to Origen, unquestionably the greatest genius among ancient Church writers. He adopted Clement's lines, extended them, and raised on them a structure of larger and fairer proportions. Quite late in his theological career, about 249—that is, on the eve of the Decian persecution, which, as he foresaw, would soon put an end to the "long peace"[1]—he wrote his principal work, a defence of Christianity from the attack directed against it, probably about seventy years before,[2] by Celsus, in a treatise called

---

[1] Orig. c. Cels. iii. 15; cp. viii. 70. When the persecution came in 250, it brought on him, at the age of sixty-seven, inflictions from which he never recovered. He died in the short interval between the death of Decius (Nov. 251) and the renewal of persecution by Gallus (cp. Euseb. vii. 1).

[2] In the latter years of Marcus Aurelius (Bigg, Bamp. Lect. p. 254); Patrick, Apol. of Origen, p. 8, even suggests A.D. 176.

the "True Discourse." In Dr. Bigg's instructive volume on "Neoplatonism"[1] will be found a very lively account of Celsus, whom Origen supposed to be at heart an Epicurean, but whom Dr. Bigg describes as "undoubtedly a Platonist," though "rather a cultivated man of the world than a philosopher."[2] Celsus had begun his work by

---

[1] Cp. also his Bampton Lectures, *l.c.*

[2] Like the sceptical pagan in the "Octavius," Celsus is a conservative as to any recognised or national *cultus*, and to such an extent as to take up a conventional or relative theory of morals (c. Cels. iv. 70; v. 27). The credulity possible among educated pagans in the second century is illustrated by his remarks (which Berkeley ridicules in the sixth dialogue of his "Alciphron") on the divining power of birds, and the religious fidelity of elephants to their oaths (iv. 88). Origen rebukes his supercilious flippancy, which in one place he calls "buffoonery" (iii. 22), and his habit of asserting without proving, etc. Yet he rises into a higher mood when he treats the idea of a universal fellowship as only too good to be true (viii. 72). He believed, not strictly in one God, but in a supreme God with intelligence and moral character; yet denied all intervention on His part in earthly affairs. He admitted a "natural tendency to sin" (iii. 63); but what would "sin" mean to him? He also believed in future rewards and punishments (iii. 16).

adopting a Jewish standpoint: in the second part he dropped this temporary mask, and stood forth in his natural position as a Pagan critic of the faith which he delighted to vilify and to represent as beneath the notice of educated minds, while yet the very bitterness of his scorn betrays a secret uneasiness as to its progress and its future. Origen follows the order which Celsus had adopted, and begins by noticing the points which a Jew was represented as likely to make by way of criticism on the Gospel narrative, as to the Virginal birth, the slaughter of the Innocents, the miracles,[1] the sufferings of One supposed to be "God" and the "Word," the humiliations of the Passion, the deprecation of the "cup," the unsatisfactory evidence, as Celsus makes his Jew regard it, of the Resurrection, etc. There

---

[1] "Supposing that they *were* wrought," Celsus compares them to effects of Egyptian occult lore; Origen points to their moral aim (c. Cels. i. 68).

is a very modern ring in two of these cavils, —that the rumour of the Resurrection originated in an excitable woman's fancy,[1] and that Jesus, had He really risen again, would have shown Himself as risen, not to a few, but to the people at large. Origen treats this sort of polemic as we might expect,[2] and calls attention to the truthfulness of the Evangelists, to the willingness of Christ's self-sacrifice, to the fulfilment of His predictions, to the moral change wrought in the Apostles, who after the Resurrection became fearless,[3] to the manifold divine purposes served by an Incarnation; and makes the telling *ad hominem* remark,

[1] C. Cels. ii. 55. Renan reproduced this suggestion by making "une hallucinée" the authoress of the Resurrection-belief. Celsus adds, "And perhaps some one else, *imagining* what he wished for."

[2] We cannot, says Origen, suppose an illusory dream in the case of persons not under the influence of delirium; and the risen Lord spared His enemies the sight of His presence, which they would not have been able to endure (c. Cels. ii. 60, 67).

[3] C. Cels. ii. 45, 56.

that Jewish objections to the Gospel statements might be turned against the Old Testament, which also demanded faith, and contained severe language. But the interest of the "Reply to Celsus" becomes much greater when the opponent is dealt with in his proper person. He had sneered at Christians as divided into parties, as not venturing to proselytise among the well-informed, but hunting for converts wherever they could find a knot of "unintelligent folk,"—of "women or children or slaves," and any others who could be coaxed or frightened into a blind credence:[1] and also

---

[1] C. Cels. i. 9; iii. 44, 49, 50, 55, 74, 75; vi. 14. Celsus goes into details as to the *status* of these proselytisers —wool-combers, leather-dressers, etc. They whisper to boys that they had better come to the women's apartments, or to this or that shop, and there learn the truth, etc. Origen says, "We are *not* so mad as to say, 'Knowledge deprives men of spiritual health;' and when we teach, we do not say, 'Attend to *me*.'" Education, he asserts, helps to the knowledge of God. So in vi. 7, he says that Scripture encourages "dialectics" (Cp. Tatian, ad Græcos, 33). On the unselfish activity of

of swelling their numbers by persons of bad character, to whom they held out imaginary hopes.[1] Origen meets the first charge by tracing the diversity of sects to mental activity in the study of Christian documents, and the second by affirming that, instead of disparaging culture, the "great Church" (as Celsus calls the Church Catholic in distinction from the sects)[2] emphasised its value, recognised its "debt both to wise and to unwise," and encouraged competent minds to use their intellects for the illustration or exposition of Christian truth,—in other words, to become theologians,—while the less gifted must necessarily assimilate truth in simpler forms.[3] And the unbeliever's

Christian propagandists, in villages and farmsteads as well as in cities, cp. Origen, c. Cels. iii. 9.

[1] C. Cels. iii. 59, 78. Gibbon makes an insidious use of this accusation (ii. 182). "He ought," says Milman, "either to have denied the moral reformation introduced by Christianity, or fairly to have investigated all its motives."

[2] C. Cels. v. 59.

[3] C. Cels. iii. 52, 74; vi. 10, 14. In i. 9, 13, he says

solicitude for moral interests is shown to be needless in view of the facts that bad men were invited by Christian teachers to adopt the best means for becoming good, but there was no preference shown for them as bad, and that they did not form more than a minority of the Christian body.[1] It was on Celsus' part a revival of the old taunt against "the friend of publicans and sinners;" and he anticipated the ethical pessimism of some moderns by almost denying the possibility of a complete reformation of character, whereupon Origen affirms that numbers have undergone such a change, and urges that God accepts repentance, or even an advance towards goodness, and that fear and hope as to the future life are that the average man must go by simple faith, but that to reason out convictions is intrinsically the higher way. Cultured converts were numerous: Pantænus is said to have been a Stoic. About the end of the "primitive" period Arnobius mentions Christian orators, grammarians, lawyers, physicians, in Adv. Gent. ii. 8.

[1] C. Cels. iii. 65. Cp. Tertull. ad Nat. i. 5.

motives morally admissible.[1] Among other "modern" points in Celsus we may note his charge of egoism against the Christian doctrine of man,[2] as if the dignity ascribed to man by Scripture were too great for a being so insignificant,—a charge, in fact, levelled against all religion : or his assumption that to believe in "miracle" is to bring a charge of imperfection against the Maker's original work;[3] or again, his contempt for the materialism of worshipping "a dead man" and expecting a bodily resurrection.[4] But to return to the complaints made by him against Christians ; they are *not*, says Origen, careless of moral discipline ; they exclude from their fellowship men known to be vicious,—where any such exist ; they are *not*

---

[1] C. Cels. iii. 68, 69, 71, 78. Cp. i. 43.

[2] C. Cels. iv. 23 ff., 74 ff. Arnobius unintentionally recurs to this position of Celsus, and attempts to promote humility by degrading humanity to the "proletariat" of creation (adv. Gent. ii. 29).

[3] C. Cels. iv. 69.   [4] C. Cels. vii. 36 ; v. 14.

factious, *not* misanthropic, *not* unfair or disrespectful towards the best philosophers; they recognise all true sayings of philosophers as from God, but they cannot ignore other language which is unworthy or inconsistent: if Plato is set up against Christ, is it possible to uphold all that is in Plato? Nor can it be said with any fairness that Christianity plagiarises from Platonism,—as, for instance, about points of moral duty, or as to the nature of future blessedness.[1] Nor, again, could Christians be fairly ranked with members of secret and unlawful societies:[2] nor were they overvaluing the body when they gave it such honour as the

---

[1] Cp. Book vi. It is curious that Celsus ascribed the Christian language about humility to "misapprehension" of some words of Plato. Origen answers that true humility is not responsible for any extravagances of visible self-abasement, for they are not the indications of its presence; and adds that "if some, through want of education, do not clearly understand our doctrine about humility, we must make allowance for" them (vi. 15).

[2] C. Cels. i. 1; viii. 20. Above, p. 177.

Christian doctrine of a future life involved : [1] nor was their faith inconsistent with a due interest in the present life, its ties, its burdens, and its duties.[2] The Incarnation did *not* imply any degradation of Deity, and did promote the moral good of humanity : [3] and the anthropomorphic or anthropopathic language of the Old Testament was simply an accommodation to the level of a childlike apprehension.[4] Allegorism is to be recognised in the interpretation of parts of its narrative : [5] it is a form, in many cases, employed to set forth moral teaching ; and general attacks on the language of prophecy

---

[1] C. Cels. viii. 50.

[2] C. Cels. viii. 55–57. He calls the single life "superior" to the married; but says, "If we wish, we will marry, and share in what life has to give, enduring its appointed evils as trials of the soul."

[3] C. Cels. iv. 5, 14, 15 ; vi. 73 ; iii. 29.

[4] C. Cels. iv. 37, 71 ff. ; vi. 62.

[5] He carries this method somewhat far (c. Cels. iv. 44, 49); and in vii. 20 ff. misapplies it in forgetfulness of the gradual character of the moral training of mankind. Yet cp. De Princip. iv. 1. 19.

are worthless, until it is *proved* to be demoralising or unmeaning; and let pagan myths be contrasted with its ethical majesty of tone. As for some wild extravagances adduced against the Church, she is nowise responsible for them; they come from heretical quarters.[1] Although some things in the Reply savour of Origen's peculiar speculations or modes of speech,[2] it contains teaching in every sense "Catholic" and healthful, to the effect that God always respects human freewill:[3] that our knowledge of Him is real, though inadequate for

---

[1] C. Cels. vi. 24–38; viii. 15. Celsus was so careless about facts as to impute to Christians in general the "Ophite" notion that the fall was a deliverance from the "obscurantist tyranny" of the Creator.

[2] *E.g.* in the direction of Universalism (c. Cels. v. 16; viii. 72); or when he uses language of an Arianizing sound (v. 37; vi. 61, 64), or restricts prayer, in the proper sense, to the worship of the Father (v. 4; viii. 13); or when, arguing *ad hominem*, he admits that even if Christ's appearance among men were Docetic, illusion might be the needful treatment of a race morally insane (iv. 19).

[3] C. Cels. iv. 70; vi. 57.

a full comprehension:[1] that the evidences for Christianity run in lines at once various and harmonious;[2] that if a man believes in Providence, he is well on the road to belief in Christ;[3] that certain things which are beyond nature in the ordinary sense of the term are within God's power, and "not contrary to nature."[4] In fact he repeatedly reminds us of our great philosophic divine, who had found a single passage of his so fruitfully suggestive:[5] the mysterious "sequences" of providential government, the mysterious diversity of human opportunities and dispositions,[6] are dwelt on as if

[1] C. Cels. vi. 62, 65; vii. 44.
[2] C. Cels. iii. 33.
[3] C. Cels. v. 3. As we should now say, a living theism finds its goal in Christianity. Clement urges that Christianity rests on such a theism (Strom. i. 52). The two statements are correlative.
[4] C. Cels. v. 23.
[5] The "sagacious observation" ascribed to Origen in the Introduction to the "Analogy" is contained in two sentences of the Philocalia, c. 2, of which Butler, in his footnote, quotes only the first. Cp. c. Cels. iv. 4.
[6] C. Cels. iv. 8; iii. 38; vi. 45.

he had habitually felt that in nature, as in grace, God's ways could be but "imperfectly comprehended;" and he expressly says, almost in Butler's phrase, that man's nature is formed for virtue.[1] He himself, too, resembles Butler in another respect,—in candour and moderation of statement; he will not, he says, oppose any fair argument, though it be used by an adversary.[2] Withal he cherishes a hope which might then perhaps seem too daring—that although Christians were still "very few" in comparison with the entire population of the empire, yet one day their faith would universally triumph. But the great general value of the treatise in regard to Apologetic is that he brings out the supreme importance of moral considerations in the estimate of a religion. He holds that the moral character of an alleged miracle belongs to the question

---

[1] C. Cels. iv. 25. Cp. Analogy, i. c. 3.
[2] C. Cels. vii. 46. Cp. i. 42.

of its evidence;[1] that the moral tone prevalent within the Church is one of her main credentials; that faith is both rational and moral;[2] that a Theism worthy of the name sustains morality. And so, as a recent writer on his "Apology" expresses it, he finds the best defence of Christianity in the person of "Christ Himself," and in the moral effects "produced by His Gospel," that is, by His living presence and energy "in the hearts and lives of men."[3]

(5.)

There is a certain affinity between the

[1] C. Cels. i. 68; ii. 51; iii. 25. De Pressensé remarks that while he does not make miracle the main ground of belief, he gives it a higher value by regarding it as the substance of Christianity, "qui n'est pas autre chose que l'intervention surnaturelle de l'amour divin pour nous sauver" (Trois Prem. Siècl. 2me 5, 11, 357).

[2] C. Cels. i. 11; iii. 40. So, too, he says (vi. 10) that the Christian teacher does not require an act of faith in the Divine Sonship until Christianity has been fairly presented to each hearer "in the manner accordant with his character and disposition."

[3] Patrick, The Apology of Origen, p. 321.

Alexandrian tone of apology and that of Marcus Minucius Felix, who seems to have written during the "long peace," shortly before the conversion of Cyprian. He puts his work into the form of a dialogue between a pagan named Cæcilius and a Christian named Octavius, on the seashore at Ostia.[1] Octavius had observed that Cæcilius, on passing an image of Serapis,[2] paid it a formal homage by kissing his own hand;[3] he expresses regret, and Cæcilius is made uneasy. By way of defending himself against the implied imputation of gross error, he enters on an elaborate plea—not indeed for a real

[1] Octavius is a friend of Minucius, and has visited him at Rome. Cæcilius joins them at Ostia. Their seaside walk on an autumn evening is charmingly described, and we are made to look on with them at boys playing "ducks and drakes" (so J. J. Blunt renders the Latin, Hist. Ch. p. 94) with shells on the shore.

[2] Clem. Alex. has much to say about Serapis, Cohort. 48. He was Apis as = Osiris, and for Greeks identified with Dionysos. His *cultus* was popular as being comprehensive.

[3] Cp. Job xxvi. 27.

belief in the gods, but for conformity to polytheistic rites or usages, on the ground that they are associated with the greatness of Rome. His own view is purely agnostic;[1] we know nothing, and can know nothing, about the causes of things; there is no trace of a guiding providence, for calamities befall good and bad alike; so that chance, most probably, rules all. In default, then, of any real knowledge on the subject, it is our wisdom to adhere to the ancient ritual as representing a universal tradition, which has given such strong support to men of all races.[2] Then he turns on the Christians as ignorant, credulous adherents of an unlawful

---

[1] "Omnia in rebus humanis dubia, incerta," etc. The result is tersely given further on: "Quod supra nos, nihil ad nos" (c. 13), agnosticism leading to "secularism."

[2] This is very like the line taken in 384 by Symmachus in his plea for the restoration of the altar of Victory (Relatio Symm. 8, ff.). Cp. Tertull. ad Nat. ii. 1, that Christianity has against her "a vast force," including "institutiones majorum . . . vetustatem, consuetudinem."

"faction," afraid to come out into the open daylight, "mute in public, talkative in corners," contemptibly foolish in sacrificing life's pleasures, and even life itself, for a wholly uncertain future; their belief is a "mad superstition," their religious usages "impious" and abhorrent;"—here he brings up, without actually committing himself to, the vilest of the libels against Christians;— their hope of resurrection is irrational;[1] their deity is conceived of as "restlessly interfering and impertinently inquisitive," and also as unjust in predetermining human conduct;[2] their habits are sullenly unsocial, their daily life darkened by stupid self-denials,[3] their ranks filled up by "unlearned

[1] The pagan gibe at "inepta solatia" (c. 11) may find a parallel in a modern positivist sneer at "moral sofas and spiritual cakes and ale."

[2] "Quidquid agimus, ut alii fato, ita vos Deo addicitis; igitur iniquum judicem fingitis" (c. 11). The allusion is to Christian language about "the elect."

[3] Here the pagan, after remarking on the absence of Christians from "spectacula," processions, and "convivia

and rustic" converts. Why will they trouble themselves about the unknowable? Why not leave uncertainties as they found them? He concludes with a tone of supercilious confidence: "Well, what has Octavius got to say in answer?" Minucius interposes, "Don't *you* be too sure before you have heard the other side;" and Octavius begins his reply by remarking on the inconsistencies of the pagan position, and on the ignoble and even "sacrilegious" indifferentism of a wilful ignorance in presence of light derivable by universal reason from the testimony of nature, of poets and philosophers, and even of every-day language,[1] to one supreme

publica," lays stress on Christians' abstention from such pleasant things as wreaths for the hair and odours for the body. "You reserve unguents for funerals; you even deny wreaths to sepulchres" (c. 12). In c. 38 Octavius explains that Christians freely enjoy the scent of flowers; as Clem. Alex. says that "to enjoy the sight of a beautiful flower is to glorify its Maker" (Pædag. ii. 70).

[1] He refers to phrases used by the common people: "God is great," and "If God grants it." This seems borrowed from Tertull. Apol. 17.

and infinite God,[1]—to a providence both general and special.[2] It is paganism, he contends, which is irrational, which turns its back upon knowledge; the belief in God is imbedded in human language, and affirmed or admitted, in one form or another, by philosophers of all schools; in fact, philosophy leads to religion.[3] Then follows a severe criticism on the absurdity of pagan myths, and pagan image-worship;[4] the power of Rome is daringly traced, not to her

---

[1] God is described as above all human comprehension, "immensus" (in sense of infinite or unlimited), "et soli sibi, tantus quantus est, notus" (c. 18). So further on: "Ex hoc Deum credimus quod eum sentire possumus."

[2] One illustration of this point is, that "if Britain sees but little of the sun, it is warmed by the sea which flows around it."

[3] Here comes the bold saying, "Any one may think aut nunc Christianos philosophos esse, aut philosophos fuisse jam tunc Christianos" (c. 20).

[4] Minucius (like Clem. Alex., Cohort. 55, and Tertull., Apol. 10) takes the "Euhemerist" view of the gods as deified men. The sarcastic description of the process by which a piece of wood or stone or metal gradually becomes a god was evidently written with a recollection of Isa. xliv. 15.

religiousness, but to her unscrupulousness;[1] the pagan system is demoralising, and Christians see evil spirits at work behind it. The false accusations are then dealt with,[2] and that which related to the murder of infants and the feasting on their flesh provokes a retort against horrible myths and human sacrifices; and as for the nonsense about the ass's head—well, what of Egyptian worship of cattle? As to the Christian community, it is *not* wholly made up of "plebeians;"[3] its strict monogamy, its fraternal unity, its worship, consisting in the oblation of a "pure heart," and the dedication of daily conduct,[4] its horror of sin even in

---

[1] This is one of the most courageous passages in Christian "Apology." *E.g.* "Quidquid Romani . . . possident, audaciæ præda est," etc. (c. 25). But Minucius is copying Tertullian (Apol. 25).

[2] Octavius owns that he once believed them (c. 28).

[3] Cp. Tertull. ad Scap. 4; Origen c. Cels. iii. 9.

[4] Speaking to a pagan, a Christian of that age would not say more about the nature of Christian worship. Octavius says nothing about actual prayers: "Qui innocentiam colit, Domino supplicat" (c. 32).

thought, its consciousness of an invisible, ubiquitous Presence, from whom no secrets are hid,[1] its contented poverty, its cheerful courage under persecution, its avoidance of "pleasures" which are in fact debasements,— are moral tokens in its favour; and at the end of this striking plea come words which summarise much: "We don't *say* great things, but we *live* them:" it is not in talk, but in conduct that the strength of our case lies. The story ends with an admission by Cæcilius that he is now convinced of the existence of God and of providence, and of the purity of Christian morals; he hopes to receive on the morrow further light on some points which are not yet clear.

In looking back at Octavius' plea, which is but an introduction to a complete apology,[2]

---

[1] "A quo nullum potest esse secretum" (c. 32). Compare the original of our Collect for Purity: "Quem nullum latet secretum."

[2] Boissier suggests that the silence of Minucius Felix about the characteristics of Christianity was part of

we see much that reminds us of Clement or of Origen, but also something of a tone which is very pronounced in Tatian with regard to the pagan gods. The vileness and folly of pagan worship are emphasised with relentless severity; its temples are declared to be haunts of vice; the awful words in which St. Paul associates it with the influence of "demons"[1] are expanded into a description of that influence as dictating oracles, as disturbing life, as torturing the bodies of the possessed, but as yielding to exorcism in the name of "the true and only God." We must not be in haste to criticise such bursts of indignation against the then dominant idolatry. If there was a time for seeing in it a pathetic evidence of the religious instinct in human nature, constraining men to seek

his plan for conciliating the educated pagans, to whom a Christian, as such, would seem "une sorte de sauvage," hostile to literature and civilisation (Fin du Paganisme, i. 334).

[1] 1 Cor. x. 20.

for their God, however blindly and erringly if haply they might feel after Him and find Him,—there was also a time for bringing out the idea which was doubtless in the Apostle's mind in the passage above referred to,—that the actual "cults" of Greek or Latin deities, not to speak of Asiatic or Egyptian, had become centres of moral pestilence, and were doing the work of the powers of evil.

(6.)

One other great name remains—the name of Tertullian. He is in one way like the Alexandrians, but also and more noticeably unlike them. The contrast shows itself chiefly in frequent disparagement of Greek literature and Greek philosophy.[1] Profes-

---

[1] It was unworthy of a Christian apologist to give currency to a stupid fiction about Plato's "gluttony" (Apol. 46). In his De Præscr. Hær. 7, Tertullian breaks out against "the wretched Aristotle," as having taught the Gnostics "dialecticam, artificem struendi et destruendi," etc. Elsewhere he flatly denies " that God

sional habits had made him a special pleader; and a harsh, vehement, absolutist temper [1] made him prone to take up extreme positions. Of "sweetness," of moderation, of balance and patience in judgment, he has very little; less than ever, naturally, when he had broken off from the communion of the Church, and become a narrow-minded intolerant schismatic. Yet he resembles Clement or Origen in one famous and pregnant sentence (often quoted, we know, by

was ever found without Christ, or that the Holy Spirit was ever brought home to any one without the sacred gift (*sacramentum*) of faith;" meaning, it would seem, apart from the actual reception of Christianity (de Anima, 1). Sometimes, he grants, philosophers have hit the mark, but this by means of a " publicus sensus, quo animam Deus dotare dignatus est" (ib. 2). Then he goes on in his usual strain: "Philosophy has lighted on this common intelligence, and inflated it by way of glorifying her own art;" she makes her own opinions law of nature, etc. And in c. 6, "No one's hesitation *de exitu animæ* has ever been abated by Plato's honey and water" (cp. above, p. 69).

[1] In the opening of his "De Patientiâ" he frankly laments his own habitual "fever of impatience."

Mr. Gladstone) on the "witness borne to Christ by the human soul" as "naturally Christian."[1] Not that he cared to find that soul "in schools of learning, or in libraries;" he would rather look for it "in crossways and workshops;" he wanted to get hold of the rough material of humanity, to talk face to face with "the man in the street,"[2]—as we might say, not with University students, but with "East End" mechanics. As De Pressensé expresses it,—even before appealing to Scripture, he produced "that immortal letter of credit for Christianity," the

---

[1] Apol. 17.

[2] De Testim. Animæ, i.: "Te (animam) simplicem et rudem et impolitam . . . compello . . . de compito, de trivio, de textrino." This strong non-academic line, however characteristically one-sided, would serve as a correction of that unchristian tendency to form an inner circle of exclusively initiated souls, which Gnostic influences, wherever felt, were likely to encourage (cp. Lightfoot on Colossians, etc., pp. 77, 98), and which, as we have seen, had proved somewhat too attractive to Clement of Alexandria. Minucius Felix follows Tertullian at some distance, avoiding declamatory phraseology, in Octav. 16.

unsophisticated "conscience" of man.[1] He felt that man was made for religion, that only in God as revealed in Christ could he find the end of his being, or appreciate the value of his life;[2] and although, too characteristically, we miss in his representation of Christ "that gentle aureole of love which is," as it had been in Clement's treatment, "the most irresistible attraction" of the figure of Christ, yet still it was the Person of that Saviour, as "the living Word, that he sought for beyond all else in the word written."[3] He pours forth all his scorn and wrath on pagan mythology, developing in much detail the identification of its gods with demons; but the parts of his great treatise which interest modern readers most are those in which he pictures the serious,

---

[1] Trois Prém. Siècl. 2me sér. ii. 471.

[2] For his view of Christ as the God-Man, cp. Apol. 21.

[3] "Perverse, in the sense of wrong-headed, he often was in his estimate of sin and of the truth; but he was never wrong-hearted" (Dict. Chr. Biogr. iv. 864).

orderly, temperate, and brotherly social life of Christians, with its discipline, its earnest and regulated worship, including intercessions for the sovereign and the Empire, — its Agapæ with their hymns and their prayers, its monthly collections for the poor and the distressed.[1] He illustrates the fact that Christian faith had stimulated the sense of human brotherhood; for he regards all mankind as united in one commonwealth. If the view of life here taken by Tertullian is not quite free from morbid elements,[2] he is much more equable and, so to speak, sensible in his estimate of a Christian's relation to civic and social life, than in his

---

[1] "A long life, a secure dominion, a safe house, brave armies, a faithful senate, a virtuous people, a world at rest, and whatever else a man or a Cæsar can desire" (Apol. 30). Cp. Clem. Rom. ad Cor. 31; and Arnobius, adv. Gent. iv. 36, "Our meetings in which peace and pardon are besought for all magistrates, armies, kings."

[2] *E.g.* "Nihil nostra refert in hoc ævo, nisi de eo quam celeriter excedere" (Apol. 41).

later or sectarian period. He even recognises the lawfulness of serving in the Imperial army;[1] he does not object to swearing by the Emperor's health, although he cannot, as a Christian, keep any terms with Cæsar-worship;[2] he must consider pagan festivals as forbidden to a worshipper of God, but

---

[1] In Ad Scap. 4. he mentions "Christian soldiers" in the army of M. Aurelius. In De Cor. 11, he indicates his opinion that no man ought to enter the army *after* his conversion to the faith. Origen, in one passage, goes so far as to say, "We do not go to war in the service of the emperor, even if he urges it, but we do so on his behalf" (*i.e.* by prayer: c. Cels. viii. 73). His objection does not rest on pagan customs as attaching to military service, but on the incompatibility, as he holds, of any blood-shedding with Christianity.

[2] Apol. 32. To swear by the emperor's health or safety was in accordance with Joseph's oath (Gen. xlii. 15); to swear by his "genius" (in the sense of a guardian quasi-deity, Hor. Ep. ii. 2. 187) was to recognise idolatry. Hence Polycarp refused to swear by his fortune (Euseb. iv. 15). Theophilus says, "You will ask me, 'Why not worship the emperor?' Because he is not made to be worshipped, but to be honoured" (ad Autol. i. 11). The worship of the emperor was in effect at once a deification of Rome and a religious bond of unity for the whole empire (cp. Ramsay, Ch. in R. Empire, p. 191).

in all matters not directly connected with idolatry—in ordinary trade and traffic, in the "enjoyment of what God has made," [1]—he says distinctly that Christians and non-Christians can meet. His enthusiasm, it must be owned, betrays him into some rhetorical flourishes as to the numerical importance of Christians—"We are but of yesterday, yet we have filled every place belonging to you" except "your temples." [2] In regard to the popular suspicions or

[1] "Nullum fructum operum ejus repudiamus: plane temperamus, ne ultra modum aut perperam utamur" (Apol. 42).

[2] Origen's language on this point is perhaps not so inconsistent as at first it seems. In C. Cels. i. 27, he says that Christianity has "gained over myriads of souls;" in ii. 13, that "one cannot see any race of men which has escaped receiving the teaching of Jesus." And when, in viii. 69, he admits that those who "now agree as touching what they shall ask of the Father are very few," he means, relatively to the whole population. Lightfoot considers that to estimate the Christians of Rome in the middle of the third century as somewhat less than one-twentieth of the inhabitants of "the City," is to "err rather on the side of excess than of defect" (Hist. Essays, p. 78; cp. Gibbon, ii. 211).

calumnies, he takes the usual line of indignant protest and denial.

(7.)

Other Apologists there were, but we must pass them over. And it must always be borne in mind that the task of "defending" the faith was deemed, as in Apostolic days, to be incumbent, in various degrees, on all who had to confess Christ before men in word, or act, explicitly or constructively; and that it was effectively discharged, in multitudinous cases, by men and women who wrote no books, but simply acted out their creed, and so "put to shame the revilers of their good manner of life in Christ;"[1] of whom it was recorded, in other and more authoritative books than those of history,

---

[1] 1 Pet. iii. 16. Cp. Athenagoras, Legat. 11: "You may find among us unlearned men, and mechanics, and old women, who, if they cannot argue for the beneficial effect of our religion, yet exhibit it in their conduct" (*i.e.* by meekness under injuries, etc.).

that "whatsoever things were true, solemn,[1] just, pure, lovable, and of good report, if there was any virtue, and if there was any praise," they "thought on these things,"—and rendered thought into life.

[1] Above, p. 144.

ADDITIONAL NOTE.

SINCE the earliest of these sheets passed through the press a justly esteemed writer, who has done excellent service in the field of our mediæval Church history, maintained in the recent Church Congress that "St. Ignatius put forward with immense emphasis a *working hypothesis*, which was at once accepted by the Church at large. Advocated with a force of conviction which asked for no support or argument on the one side, or any appeal to precedent or even to Apostolic authority on the other, it was adopted as a practical theory that exactly met the needs of the case" (*Guardian*, Sept. 28, 1898, p. 1499). Dr. Jessopp's "hypothesis" could not fail to suggest difficulties. It was not easy, for instance, to understand how a sane man (of however enthusiastic a temperament) could propound with iteration to various groups of readers a "working hypothesis" without thinking himself obliged to argue in its behalf. To be sure, it may well be said that he was "too near death to argue" (H. S. Holland, The Apostolic Fathers, p. 133); but he was also too near death to care about a "working hypothesis." We mistake the man if we suppose that on the very verge of martyrdom he could throw such a passion of energy into the "advocacy" of anything that was not to him a matter of solemn fact, involving imperative obligations, and associating itself with the Divine mind and will. Nor, again, could it seem probable that in a matter so sacredly momentous as the future administration of Christ's visible kingdom and household, all Christians should "at once" accept the opinion of a single Syrian bishop as to which of several "theories" would be "practically" the most applicable to the conditions of their time. Still less, if possible, could the suggestion be thought to fit in with language in which Ignatius, being then so "near," as he says, "to God," does not hesitate to claim for the episcopal authority a representative relation to God or to Christ, or to speak of "the bishops who have been appointed," or "definitely stationed, in the furthest parts of the world," an expression showing, as Lightfoot says, that he was "contemplating regions as distant as Gaul on the one hand, and Mesopotamia on the other" (Note on Ign. Eph. 3).

But it is needless to say more, since this new view of the Ignatian position drew forth a comment from one of the hearers, the Archbishop of Canterbury himself (*Guardian*, p. 1461). "The writer of the paper seemed to think that Ignatius, when he spoke of the authority of the bishops, and called on all to obey, was creating a new state of things. He" (Archbishop Temple) "could not understand anybody reading Ignatius and not coming to the opposite conclusion. The growth of the episcopate was certainly a very difficult problem; but it was quite certain that the episcopate was in full vigour very soon after the end of the first century, and he believed that it existed before" (as to which see Bishop Lightfoot's words quoted above, p. 36).

A few words may here be added on some other points. Any reader who, like the writer, is conscious of deep obligations to Bishop Ellicott in regard to theology and exegesis, may deem it an omission not to have referred to his remarks on Luke xxiv. 23 in combination with John xx. 21 (Huls. Lectures on Life of Our Lord, pp. 397, 401). He thinks that it "cannot positively be decided" whether those who were "with" the ten apostles on the first Easter-day evening received the Holy Spirit along with them, "as St. John only uses the general term μαθηταί." (At the same time, that term is clearly used by St. John in xiii. 5, 22; xviii. 1, etc., for the apostles alone.) The bishop, however, concludes that the apostles were "the only recipients; the ἀπαρχή of the Spirit is received by the ἀπαρχή of the Church;" and the power conveyed by the whole address of Our Lord on this occasion "was an essential adjunct to their office as the ambassadors of Christ, and more especially as *the rulers of the Church.* . . . The gift" (of the Spirit) "was not general, like that at the Pentecost, but special and peculiar." That Cleopas and his companion in the walk to and from Emmaus, and those whom they "found in company with" the apostles, should then have been witnesses of an inauguration in which, as believers, they had so deep an interest, can surely cause no difficulty. Cp. also Luke vi. 17–20. (I have referred to this in The Law of Faith, p. 340.)

It may also be worth observing that the action of the *Church*, not merely of the celebrant, in the Eucharist, is clearly recognised, and even emphasised, by Bossuet. After affirming that as the consecration takes place " en la personne de Jésus-Christ, c'est lui veritablement et qui consacre et qui offre" (*i.e.* in order to "apply" the efficacy of this perfect sacrifice made "une fois" on the cross), he says, as to the plural verb *offerimus*, " Le prêtre ne fait rien de particulier que tout le peuple ne fasse conjointement, avec cette seule différence, que le prêtre le fait comme ministre public, et au nom de toute l'Eglise" (Nouvelle Explication donnée au ministre Ferry: Œuvres, xxv. 113). It is true that when Bossuet thus wrote in July, 1666, he was not as yet "the Eagle of Meaux;" but he was dean of Metz Cathedral, and a divine of sufficient mark to be carrying on what was called a "projet de réunion des protestants de France à l'Eglise catholique." It might be thought that this "eirenic" aim had led him to minimise his Church's doctrine; but at any rate in the sentence last quoted he seems to say no more than is involved in the words *sed et plebs tua sancta*, quoted above (p. 95) from the very prayer, "Unde et memores," on which he is commenting. See the *Responsio* of the present Archbishops of Canterbury and York to the bull *Apostolicæ Curæ* (c. 11, and cp. ib. c. 15, 19), where "sacerdos," "sacerdotes nostri," and "sacerdotium" are freely used in regard to the instrumental relation of the Ministry to the living and worshipping Church on the one hand, and the living and grace-bestowing Christ on the other.

It was not to the purpose of the third address to go fully into the question of Ebionism. But it may be permissible here to refer to a learned and interesting volume called an "Illustration of the Method of explaining the New Testament," etc., published in 1797 by W. Wilson, Fellow of St. John's College, Cambridge, and reprinted at the Cambridge University Press in 1838. The author devotes several chapters to the consideration of the claims set up for "Unitarianism" to represent the original Christology. He takes the familiar points as to Eusebius' evident satisfaction with the doctrinal position of the Hebrew-Christian bishops of Jerusalem, and of Hegesippus, and his appeal to an unnamed author against the Artemonite pretensions (see above, p. 127). There is indeed a well-known difficulty in Origen's identification of "the Jews who believed in Jesus" with "the Ebionites" (c. Cels. ii. 1); but Mr. Wilson interprets him as referring to "those who continued mere Jews by remaining unmixed with other Christians," *i.e.* who stood apart as a sect, and proceeds to dwell on the taunt repeatedly directed by Celsus through his "Jew" against the Jewish Christians as actually believing Jesus to be "God"—even as Dorner notes the significant fact that Celsus never taxes "the later Christianity" with having corrupted the older by the invention of that belief. Elsewhere, as we have seen, Origen describes the two classes of "Ebionite" Psilanthropists, as Eusebius does in H. E. iii. 27; and until we pass beyond Eusebius, the account of the strictly Judaical Ebionism causes no difficulty. As Dr. Hort observes (Judaistic Christianity, p. 199), it is Epiphanius who confuses us by distinguishing "Nazaræans" from Ebionites, while yet he does not feel able to say whether the "Nazaræans" believed the virginal birth, or whether their copy of St. Matthew contained the "genealogy" or no (Hær. 29. 7, 9). The distinction is unknown to earlier writers; and Dr. Hort thinks that the one sect, with its "two grades of Christological doctrine," may have been known in ante-Nicene times not only by the name which seemed to claim for them the benediction pronounced on the poor, and which was variously misunderstood by Church writers, but also by that local title which recalls a clause in the speech of Tertullus (Acts xxiv. 5); and that it probably came into existence after Hadrian, in 135, had excluded the Jews from the sacred site of Jerusalem. When this link was broken, "the men like Hegesippus, the maintainers of St. James's tradition," naturally drew nearer and nearer to the great Gentile churches; and such a step on their part "would only the more drive the Judaizers into isolation," and into accentuation of their dislike for the Pauline Christology, a dislike which may indeed have been growing into positive aversion while the Judaic-Gnostic Cerinthus was maintaining, about the close of St. John's life, that Jesus was merely the son of Joseph and Mary, on whom a heavenly power called Christ descended at His baptism. The distinction thus made between Jesus and Christ is a sort of testimony to the prevalence of a high Christology among Christians. The abrupt commencement of the homily called the second epistle of Clement (and ascribed by Lightfoot to a writer of about 120–140), appears to be aimed at the Ebionites, who were openly refusing to "think of Jesus Christ as of God," and to whom Justin alludes in the Dialogue with Trypho. It is observable that Eusebius while condemning some "lengthy" Pseudo-Clementine writings as heterodox (iii. 38), does not trace them (as we have now learned to do) to a second school of Ebionites, not unnaturally desirous of enriching from other sources their own drily negative creed. Lightfoot considers that this movement of thought had been "stealthily" going on ever since A.D. 70 (Dissertations, p. 82), but Hort assigns to it a considerably later date (Judaistic Christianity, p. 201).

The writer of an interesting paper in the *Guardian* of September 21, 1898 (p. 1438), gives cogent reasons for not accepting Professor Ramsay's view that 1 Peter was written as late as about 80 A.D. (that is, in the first or second year of Titus), when the Flavian dynasty was carrying on the policy of persecution which had been adopted by Nero. "There is," he says, "no evidence but hypothesis for a persecution on any considerable scale between the time of Nero and of Domitian," while there is strong evidence against it. But his treatment of 1 Pet. iv. 14–16 may be deemed less satisfactory. He argues that "to suffer as a Christian" is a phrase which any Christian writer of that age would use as to persecution under any "pretext;" and "it is simple to imagine Christians in Nero's reign charged with murder, robbery, etc., as pretexts for punishing their Christianity." But the case is not quite so "simple;" for St. Peter draws a clear antithesis between "suffering as a murderer," or otherwise as a criminal in the ordinary sense, and "suffering as a Christian." And as in the first member of this antithesis we are dealing with charges which are real, not with mere pretexts to cover a different motive for the infliction of punishment, so, one would think, it must be in the second. The words in 1 Pet. iii. 16 refer to the disproof, even in hostile eyes, of false imputations popularly brought against Christian conduct; and the very next words show that Christians might expect to "suffer for well doing," *i.e.* for religious fidelity, literally, "*while* doing well." The epistle may well have been written after the horrible scenes of A.D. 64, and when provincial magistrates were beginning practically to assume that the mere profession of Christianity implied hostility to social order and probable complicity in some form of gross crime. And it gains a new interest if we suppose it to have been sent by St. Peter to Pauline and other churches in Asia Minor after St. Paul's martyrdom (Dr. Swete, Gospel of St. Mark, p. xvii., and Dr. Hort, On 1 Peter, p. 6). But it may have been written while St. Paul was in Spain.

INDEX

A

Abercius, epitaph of, 102, 110
Acts, account of the Church in the, 6
Agape, the, 107, 149, 168, 250
Agnostics, pagan, 169, 239
Alexamenos, 152, 169
Alexander of Abonoteichos, 155
Alexander Severus, 77, 198
Alexandria, a centre of studies, 216; catechetical school of, 215; episcopate at, 46; persecution at, 172, 189
Allegorism, 221, 233
"Altar," use of the term, 111
Ambrose, 109
Amusements, public, 162
Anencletus, 37
"Angels" of churches, 35
Anicetus, 121
Antenicenes, questionable language of some, 131
Antioch, council of, 82
Antoninus Pius, 183
Apollonius, martyr, 164
Apollonius of Tyana, 156
"Apologetic," 201
Apostates, 189
Apostles, relation of, to Christ, 14; position of, in the earliest church, 19 ff., 137
Aristides, 205
Arles, council of, 89, 92
Arnobius, 143, 230, 231, 250
Art, associated with paganism, 159

Artemon, 127, 259
Athanasius, 78, 80
Atheism, Christians charged with, 4, 166
Athenagoras, 167, 212, 253
Atonement, doctrine of, 123, 210
Augustine, 73, 90, 106, 118

B

Baptism, belief as to, 101; ritual of, 103; of infants, 103; by laymen, 69; of "blood," 193
Basilicas, origin of, 152
Bishop, a primitive, relation of, to his people, 81 ff.; to the Church, 84
Butler, points of likeness to, in Origen, 235

C

Callistus, 74, 138, 164
Carthage, councils of, 87, 91
Catacombs, 6, 164
Catechumens, 103
Celsus, 225 ff.
Cerinthianism, 127, 260
Chrism, 105
Christ, effects of belief in, as divine, 123, 147
Christians, early, not understood by Pagans, 3; numbers of, 252
Christology, the early, 129

Church, theories as to origin of the, 7 ff.
Circus games, 162
Clement of Alexandria, 42, 45, 103, 142, 148; as apologist, 216 ff., 248
Clement of Rome, epistle of, 37, 60 ff., 76, 134
"Clinics," 94
Commission, the apostolic, 14 ff., 257
Commodianus, 136
Commodus, 181
Compromise, Christians tempted to, 165
Confirmation, 104
Corinth, character of church of, 44, 54, 60
Cornelius of Rome, 74, 92
Creed, primitive types of, 129; relation of a, to life, 124
Cross, sign of the, 159, 169
Culture, among Christians, 230
Custom, pagans' appeal to, 222, 239
Cyprian, 74 ff., 82 ff., 96, 103, 136, 139, 191

D

Decius, 181, 184
Demetrius of Alexandria, 72
Democracy, the earliest Church not a, 39, 62
Departed, prayer for the, 115
Despotism, apostolic rule not a, 52; nor Cyprian's, 84
Diognetus, epistle to, 141, 209
Dionysius of Alexandria, 112, 150, 156, 172, 185, 189, 196
Dionysius of Corinth, 43, 138
Diotrephes, 24
Disaffection, Christians charged with, 164
"Disciplina arcani," 167, 243
Discipline, 73, 98, 137, 231
Docetism, 126
Domitian, 178
Domitilla, 164, 178

E

Ebionism, 125, 128, 133, 259
Election of bishops and clergy, 77
Emperor, Christians in household of the, 152, 198; worship of the, 178, 251
Ephesus, church of, in St. Paul's time, 30
Epiphanius, 127, 259
Episcopacy, gradual growth of, 33, 43, 47
"Episkopoi," early use of the term, 28, 116
"Establishment," lay status under, 95
Eucharist, the Holy, belief as to, 105, 109; celebration of, 113; sacrifice in, 64, 70, 113, 257
Eusebius, 69, 80, 102, 127, 133, 136
Eutychius, 47
"Evangelists," 27, 34
"Exomologesis," 139
External, the, relation of, to the internal, 10

F

Fabian, bishop of Rome, 74
Faction, Christians charged with being a, 164, 240
Failings and sins among early Christians, 135
Faith, principle of, 223
Fasting, 118
Firmilian, 45
Flavius Clemens, 163, 178
Flight from persecution, 195
Fronto, 169

G

Gallienus, 179
"Genius of the Emperor," Christians refuse to swear by, 169, 251

Glabrio, Acilius, 151, 164
Gladiatorial games, 162
Gnostics, 113, 248
God, exclusive of "gods," 171
Guilds, Roman, 5

H

Hadrian, 179, 183
Happiness of early Christians, 145
Hegesippus, 42, 128, 258
Heretics' baptism, question of, 91
Hermas, 40, 118, 131, 135, 137, 148, 184, 188
Hermias, 206
Higher classes, Christians in the, 151, 163, 243
"Hippolytean" canons, 46, 77, 115
Hippolytus, 45
Hours of Communion, 106, 168
Humanity, sense of a common, 143, 165, 250

I

Idealising tone, an, 220
Idolatry, ubiquitous, 158; demoralising, 159, 214, 243, 245
Ignatius, on episcopacy, etc., 41, 255; on divinity of Christ, 126; on the Eucharist, 109
Ignorance, Christians charged with trading on, 228
"Illicit" religions, 173
Imprisonment, misery of, 190
Incarnation, doctrine of, 10, 100, 126, 205, 210, 233
Informers discouraged, 179
Institutions, congenial to Christianity, 100
Instrumentality, principle of, 11, 258
Intellect, Christian use of, 229
"Invisible Church" theory discredited, 8

Irenæus, on episcopacy, 41, 45; on the Eucharist, 112; on the Roman church, 122

J

James, "the Lord's brother," position of, at Jerusalem, 24, 37
Jerome, 46, 72
Jerusalem, council of, 54, 117
John, St., relation of episcopacy to, 36
Judaism, an "allowed" religion, 173; polemic of, 226
Judaizers, the, 125, 128
Julian, 156
Justin Martyr, 102, 109, 141, 167, 260; as apologist, 205 ff.

K

Kingdom of God, relation of the, to the Church, 7
Kinsfolk betraying Christians, 171
Knowledge of God, 223, 234

L

Laity, *status* of primitive, 57 ff.
Lapsed, question as to the, 85, 90, 191
"Libellatics," 93, 197
Libels against Christians, 4, 167, 215, 240, 243
Liturgy, primitive form of, 114
Lucian, 149, 167, 196
Lyons, persecution at, 172, 180

M

Macrianus, 156
Magic, popular belief in, 155, 226
Magisterial office, Christians' difficulties as to, 161

Magistrates, attitude of pagan towards Christians, 185
Malchion, 80
Marcus Aurelius, 155, 180, 192, 212
Married life among Christians, 148
Martyrs, 191
Means of grace, principle of, 48
Melito, 172, 212
Military service, Christians' difficulties as to, 161, 251
Ministry, two alternative theories of, 10, 49; relation of, to spiritual interests, 11
Minucius Felix, 162, 170, 238 ff., 244, 248
Mithraism, 157
Mixed chalice, the, 110
Mobs, fury of, against Christians, 166, 172
"Monarchia," the, 130
Monogamy, 243
Montanism, 41, 66, 71, 79, 195
Moral change wrought in lives by the faith, 134, 141 ff., 230

N

Natalius, 75
Natural virtues fostered by faith, 143
"Nazaræans," 259
Neoplatonism, 156
Nero, 176, 183
Noetus, 126
Novatian, 74, 94

O

Oblation, see Eucharist
"Obstinacy," 191
Ordination, qualifications for, 76
Organisation, 10
Origen, 72, 78, 83, 103, 133, 136, 138, 143, 147, 167, 234, 259; as apologist, 226 ff.

P

Pagan world, unhappiness of the, 151
Pagans, intimacy of Christians with, 166, 188; hostility of educated, to Christianity, 170
Panlænus, 216, 230
Paschal controversy, the, 80, 119 ff.
Papias, 45
Paul, St., apostolic action of, 23, 54; devotion of, to Christ, 125; on ministry, 11; relation of to "apologetic," 202
Paul of Samosata, 133
Penitents, classification of, 140
Persecutions, the official, 173 ff.; good effect of, 198
Pestilence, self-devotion in time of, 149
Peter, St., 16, 18, 20, 53; first epistle of, 174, 181, 201, 260
"Philanthropy" of Christians, 143
Philip, the emperor, story about, 139
Philosophy, varying attitude of Christians towards, 206, 209, 211, 214, 219, 232, 242, 246
Platonism, 220, 225, 232
"Pleasures," Christians reproached for abstaining from, 163, 240
Pliny the younger, 107, 123, 150, 178, 186, 192
Polycarp, 43, 120, 135, 187, 251
Pomponia Græcina, 164
Poor, collections for the, 6, 149, 250
Praxeas, 126, 129
Preaching by laymen, 72
Presbyters, 28, 45; large power of, 37, 74
Present life, Christians' attitude towards the, 233, 252
Priesthood, of the baptized, 58 ff., 88; ministerial, 59, 257

Prisca (Priscilla), 151
Propagandism, Christian, 229
Prophecy, appeal to, 213
Prophesying, gift of, 34, 71
Pseudo-Clementine books, 129, 206, 260
Psilanthropism, 127, 130, 259
Pudens, 151

Q

Quadratus, 205
Quartodecimans, 120

R

Reason, moral, Christian appeal to the, 56, 204
Relaxation of tone in time of peace, 136, 188, 198
Renunciations, baptismal, 103, 150
"Representative," sense of, as applied to ministry, 59
Rome, early church of, 37, 42, 121, 122

S

Sabbath, the, abrogated, 117
Sabellianism, 126
"Sacerdos," use of the term, 89
Sacerdotalism, 49, 64, 68
Sacraments, relation of, to the Incarnation, 123; to the idea of ministry, 48
"Sacramentum," as a sacred pledge, 150
Saturday, varying observance of, 118
Scepticism in educated Romans, 154, 170, 239
Schoolmasters, difficulties of Christian, 160
Scillitan martyrs, 186
"Seal," use of the term, 102
Sects, number of Christian, 229
Serapis, 242

Seriousness of Christian life, 144
"Seven," appointment of the, 20
Severus, 183
Sin, Christian idea of, 145, 157
Slavery, how affected by Christianity, 142, 149
Sonship, the Divine, 129 ff.
Station-days, 118
Stewardship, the ministry a, 15, 48
Stoicism, 180
"Subordinatio Filii," 131
Succession, principle of ministerial, 39
Sufferers, active charity of Christians toward, 148
"Suffragium," sense of, 77
Sulpicius Severus, 177
Superstition, in the Pagan revival, 155, 225
Sympathy between clergy and laity, 57
Synods, constitution of, 80, 87, 92

T

Tacitus, 4, 175
Tatian, 168, 211, 245
"Teaching of Apostles," the, 34, 115
Tertullian, 66, 76, 79, 101, 103, 116, 130, 135, 138, 142, 148, 160 ff., 186, 188, 192; as apologist, 246
Theatres demoralising, 162
Theodotus, 127
Theological study encouraged, 229
Theophilus, 167, 212, 251
Timothy, position of, at Ephesus, 31
Titus in Crete, 31
Torture, 190
Trade, Christians' relation to, 160, 252
Trajan, 5, 178, 183
Trinity, doctrine of the, 130

U

Unity, the Divine, 130

V

Valens, presbyter, 133
Valerian, 156, 198
Valerius of Hippo, 73
Veracity, a virtue of Christians, 147
Vespasian, 178
Victor, 121
Vienne, 167, 180

W

Wives, converted, influence of, 142
Wonders, a craving for, not the cause of spread of Christianity, 154
Word, Justin's doctrine of the, 207; other writers on the, 130, 213

Z

Zephyrinus, 75, 138

www.ingramcontent.com/pod-product-compliance
Lightning Source LLC
Chambersburg PA
CBHW031940230426
43672CB00010B/1989